THE
OVERSTREET
Comic Book
GRADING GUIDE

Dedicated to the memory of
B. McGregor

•THE•
OVERSTREET
COMIC BOOK
GRADING GUIDE

First Edition

BOOKS FROM 1930s—PRESENT INCLUDED

FULLY ILLUSTRATED WITH A COMPLETE GLOSSARY

By

ROBERT M. OVERSTREET
and GARY M. CARTER

SPECIAL CONTRIBUTORS TO THIS EDITION
Bruce Hamilton, Susan Cicconi and Mark Wilson

SPECIAL ADVISORS TO THIS EDITION
*Bruce Hamilton   *Hugh O'Kennon   *John Snyder
*Jerry Weist   *Jim Payette   *Mark Wilson   *Harry Thomas

GENERAL ADVISORY COMMITTEE TO THIS EDITION
*Dave Anderson *Terry Stroud   *Ron Pussell   *Steve Geppi   *John Verzyl
*Joe Rainone   *Erik Andresen   *Michael Naiman   *Susan Cicconi
*Harry Matetsky   *Sean Linkenback   *David Noah   *Joe Dungan
*Joe Mannarino   *Tony Starks   *Chris Lennen   *Harley Yee
*Gary Dolgoff   *Gary Colabuono   *Tom Horvitz   *Steve Carey

The CONFIDENT COLLECTOR

AVON BOOKS ◆ NEW YORK

Serious Comic Book Collectors, Don't Miss
THE OVERSTREET COMIC BOOK PRICE GUIDE
By Robert M. Overstreet
A Confident Collector™ Title from Avon Books

Front cover art: Showcase #4, September/October 1956. Copyright © 1956 DC Comics Inc. Copyright renewed 1984 DC Comics Inc. All rights reserved. Used by permission of DC Comics Inc.

Cover shows an infinity projection of the first Silver Age appearance of The Flash, Showcase #4.

THE OVERSTREET COMIC BOOK GRADING GUIDE (1st Edition) is an original publication of Avon Books.

AVON BOOKS
A division of
The Hearst Corporation
1350 Avenue of the Americas
New York, New York 10019

Copyright © 1992 by Robert M. Overstreet
Published by arrangement with Overstreet Publications Inc.
Library of Congress Catalog Card Number: 91-92479
ISBN: 0-380-76910-7

The Confident Collector is a trademark of Avon Books.

First Avon Books Trade Printing: May 1992

AVON TRADEMARK REG. U.S. PAT OFF. AND IN OTHER COUNTRIES, MARCA REGISTRADA, HECHO EN U.S.A.

Printed in the U.S.A.

10 9 8 7 6 5 4 3 2 1

TABLE OF CONTENTS

Acknowledgements 6

Forward, by Bruce Hamilton 7

By Way of Introduction 9

Why Is Grading So Important? 10

The Evolution of Comic Book Grading 12

Using This Grading Guide 15

The Comic Book Grading Card ....color section,18

How To Describe Comic Book Condition 17

Diagram Of A Comic Book 19

Restoration Notes by Susan Cicconi............................20

Comic Book Restoration by Mark Wilson 29

A Word About Mail Order 33

Grade: Mint begins...34

Grade: Near Mint begins 68

Grade: Very Fine begins 97

Grade: Fine begins...130

Grade: Very Good begins 168

Grade: Good begins..216

Grade: Fair begins 255

Grade: Poor begins 283

Glossary 291

Cross Index of comic book covers 302

ACKNOWLEDGEMENTS

The authors would like to thank the following for their inspirited advice, support and loyalty: Dottie Harris, Lasker Harris, Martha Overstreet, Lisa Carter, John and Linda Snyder, Bruce and Helen Hamilton, Jim and Lynda Payette, Mark Wilson, Harry and Carol Thomas, Jerry Weist, Hugh O'Kennon, David Noah, Sonny Johnson, Jeff Overstreet and Tony Overstreet.

We would also like to thank Susan Cicconi and Mark Wilson for their articles on restoration and to Bruce Hamilton for his forward.

FORWARD
By
BRUCE HAMILTON

Juan Ponce de Leon, the Spanish explorer, sought the perfect life and searched Florida for the "Fountain of Youth." He failed to find it, of course. Throughout history, man's frustrating quest for perfection has woven through all facets of his life, blanketing his work, his play, and his dreams. The teenage boy lusts for a nubile, perfect "10" girl; churches fill with parishioners looking for a pathway to heaven; peddlers hope to win salesman-of-the-year awards; the housewife shops for fruit with no bruises; Olympians train for years to set best-ever records; the wealthy spend thousands on a watch that tells time no better than a $39.95 model; students stay up all night cramming for an examination, hoping to score a perfect 100.

Collectors, too, have been searching for perfection since collecting began, looking for their treasures from antiquity, hoping to find them in mint, like-new condition. But what *is* mint? How is a collector to know it when he sees it? Is it possible to arrive at a formula to know what to pay for mint or does it justify whatever you can afford? Bob Overstreet and Gary Carter's new Grading Guide will, I think, fill your head with new perspectives on the hobby and should help you to come to some of your own answers to the perplexing questions I've posed. It has for me.

It's been fascinating over the years to watch the definition of mint change in the comic book marketplace. In the 1960s, comics were either collectible or uncollectible, and the condition most dealers were satisfied to describe, was that their desirable copies were in "good or better." I asked a well-known East Coast dealer why he didn't specify the condition of his comic books in more detail. His response was, "What do you expect me to do? Sit down and grade every one? I've got thousands of them for sale. It would take days." Mint was a coin-dealer's term that he didn't think should apply to comic books. But there were already some collectors — and a few dealers — who thought differently.

Fans would rifle through newsstand racks for the latest comics in those days, pick out the best copies and say, "Ah, these are surely mint!" Then they began to seek older books that looked like their new ones. For every collector who wanted mint comics and would pay more to obtain that rare, elusive "perfect" condition, a dealer popped up who would obligingly help him find them. And the debates began.

Collectors started to compare their mint comics, soon concluding that if they had two mint comic books and one was better than the other, then one was not mint. This is to presuppose the position that many held: mint means perfect, better than like new: an unattainable goal. Is this what collectors should seek — the impossible? I think not. It only seems reasonable that the best available, the best *possible*, should be the goal. Then, one questions, why not call that mint?

Conscientious dealers — and I was one of them — steadfastly have refused to grade anything above *near* mint. I remember with some irony a time when I was selling copies from one of the legendary top-grade collections that surfaced in the 1970s, the best of which I described as only "near mint." There was a collector at the time from the Midwest named Pennack, who had such a reputation for fussiness in his quest for mint comic books, that dealers who sold them to him coined the phrase, "Pennack perfect," to describe anything he would buy. Pennack wouldn't respond to my ads offering the near mints,

7

but a Texas dealer did buy from me and resold the same comics to Pennack, who later touted them as being some of the choicest in his collection. It was a sobering experience.

As suggested elsewhere in this volume, chaos is the natural order of things, including the deterioration of comic books. Being what they are, their deterioration begins during the process of printing and continues through binding, distribution, selling, handling, reading, and eventually by just keeping, aging in the passage of time. If all comic books were in perfect condition and remained that way — impervious to damage — would the old ones be worth anything today? Would the hobby itself, in fact, even exist? Is it not true, after all, that those things we value most are only temporal or fragile: a flower, a sunset, a perfect day, life itself?

How great it would be, a chorus of voices will likely shout, if all comics were perfect and prices thereby remained low! We would all be able to afford to go out and buy, cheaply, what we wanted. "Oh, happy day!" Johnny Mercer penned in the lyrics to the musical, **Li'l Abner**. But the real world doesn't work that way. There would be no dealers to seek them out to sell and, alas, I'm afraid by this time, most would have already been thrown away by their original owners.

As life isn't perfect, there are no perfect comic books. So, is a grading guide needed and why hasn't there been one before? The answers are yes, and because the hobby wasn't ready for one. Now, I believe, it is. A 100-point grading guide suggests a comparison to academic achievement where a 90-point average is high and acceptable. When Bob and Gary analyzed their task it was clear some rethinking had to be done. Should mint really be perfect, or should it reflect a range from the best known to anything better than that, accepting that "up" has no known limit?

It's been amusing to watch Bob and Gary as they developed this book. Both are obsessive collectors who approached the task with the same relentless pursuit as they do their hobby, to compile a nearly perfect book. In time, they'll be the first to find flaws and someday will surely issue a revised edition.

When I saw what these scholars had done I loved it. Quickly, I accepted that a range of 98-100 can and should be termed mint. That leaves 100 as the unattainable goal. The best copies known of vintage comics should have a top classification, and somehow "near mint" doesn't quite cut it. I freely admit that this 20-20 vision comes from the hindsight of having read this guide. As far as the usage of the word "mint," I don't have any trouble with that at all, for the term has become generic, and despite the fact that coins are minted, stamps and comics are printed and automobiles are manufactured, everybody understands when you call perfect examples of anything mint. Let's put that issue to rest.

Now let's grade the guide. I think it's needed and is going to become a useful tool for collectors in many areas, not just comic books. The problems with grading are faced head-on in this volume and we can thank Bob Overstreet and Gary Carter for making it happen.

BY WAY OF INTRODUCTION

Since earliest times humans have attempted to achieve two goals. One is to win, by being or owning the best. The other is the quest for perfection, whether it be the ideal of the ancient Greeks, renaissance art, or comic book appreciation. These factors have led us to a rather enigmatic pursuit; an interest in obtaining comic books not just for their historical importance, entertainment value, and artistic/literary achievement. The vast majority of comic book collectors also understand, appreciate, and value their state of preservation!

Appreciating the level of preservation in physical objects is as old as the understanding of the law of entropy. This law suggests that physical objects deteriorate with time because of "use" and exposure to the elements. Understanding this natural law allows us to draw conclusions important in understanding why so many view grading as such a critical component of comic book collecting. Specimens in a high state of preservation are almost always rarer than specimens in a lesser state of preservation. Because there are fewer of them, they are harder to locate and obtain. Inextricably linking condition with value, the law of supply and demand also dictates that an item in a high grade will be worth more than its multitude of lesser condition cousins. This is because there will not be enough of them to fill demand.

Some collectors care little about condition. To these purists go the admiration of many. For the rest of the comic book collecting world, condition is all important and is a compelling and driving force, motivating fans to scour conventions, shops, and advertisements in search of this elusive commodity.

This search often leads to disappointment because what one person describes as "really great shape" or "just like new," another person describes as "uncollectible," a difference in evaluative criteria that is to be expected. Every collectible in history has encountered this same challenge.

In our global culture, enthusiasts commonly buy, sell, and trade comic books using condition as a key factor in determining price. Collectors and dealers who describe the state of preservation by long distance communication face a number of challenges, the least of which is bias about the importance of defects. This variability is easier to understand when one considers that *comic books are, by far, the most complicated of all paper collectibles to grade!* Defects impact different collectors in different ways. For some, page whiteness may be the most important esthetic factor, while structural perfection may be the preference of another. The quirks of perception have bewildered, frustrated, and even angered novice and experienced collectors since the 1950s, so much so in fact, that many hobbyists have come to accept grading incongruities as unavoidable. Even seasoned veterans hold vastly different opinions on the subtle differences between grade ranges, thus the need for usable, practical, and standardized criteria for grading.

In the late 1970s, the idea of a comic book grading guide was first discussed by the authors and a commitment was made in 1987 to begin the task. By 1990, with the need for a grading guide becoming acute, The Overstreet Price Guide added greater definition to its grading standards by rewriting all grade definitions and adding sub-grades. This transition was climaxed by the development of a 100 point system, a page whiteness level system, and the publication of this book.

When one reads this grading guide, we feel it is important to keep three concepts in mind. First, this guide is not intended to cover every defect. There are thousands of defects that can occur in thousands of combinations! This edition illustrates only the most common and the most important defects, and provides insight as to their place in the overall grading scheme.

Second, this volume has been designed to offer everyone instruction and information, regardless of his level of experience and expertise.

And third, The Overstreet Comic Book Grading Guide is neither an expression of the strictest nor the most lenient grading practices. Instead, it represents a reasonable average of the grading practices throughout the country. As with all averages, it is possible that any collector's or dealer's standards may or may not vary from those proposed here. Whatever the case, please be assured that much time, effort, and research was put into this publication to ensure fairness and accuracy. As you peruse the various sections, we hope you will be rewarded with new ideas and insights. Exploring the often complex and always fascinating world of grading comic books will surely enhance your appreciation of those magical tickets to fantasy.

Robert M. Overstreet
Gary M. Carter
1991

WHY IS GRADING SO IMPORTANT?

In the world of collectibles, there are few universals. The individual agendas of collectors are as varied as there are kinds of collectibles. Collectors may want items related to historical events or periods. They may seek out things that are traditionally famous or be totally motivated by internal needs that only they understand. Collectors may frantically attempt to recapture their childhood with items they actually possessed as youngsters or with items they wanted to possess as children but somehow were never able to acquire. But among all the myriad individual collecting criteria, one thing has emerged as a "universal" concept. Whether it be antique furniture or match book covers, coins or stamps, big little books or comics, the vast majority of enthusiasts want the items they collect to be as close to the original condition of manufacture as possible. This key idea may seem painfully obvious to those who have been comic book collectors for a while. But to those newly arrived on the scene, it might not be quite so obvious.

To gain even more insight into why condition continues to be the "Holy Grail" of comic collectors, consider the law of entropy. This "law" suggests that the natural order is for things to deteriorate from a state of order to a state of chaos; to literally decay, from a well ordered state, back to the original elemental particles. So it goes with comic books. The "deterioration" or aging process of comic books can be better understood by investigating "the nature of the beast" so to speak. Comic books are fundamentally a mechanical device. That is, comic books, as with all books, are intended to move. They move every time we open them to read the print and look at the pictures inside.

The mechanical device concept is often overlooked and yet is one of the most important reasons that comics seem to age so quickly. The flexible paper that is used in the manufacture of comic books is a double-edged sword. On the one hand, its flexibility allows the mechanical object to work. On the the other hand, the flimsy assemblage of fragile materials hovers on the edge of destruction with every reading. This "Catch 22" is often the source of philosophical and passionate debate among collectors. If one enjoys a comic by using it for the original purpose it was manufactured for, the *de facto* result is a reduction in condition, even with the most careful reading techniques. Not only that, but, ironically for collectors, no matter how carefully one handles comic books, they age anyway.

Another factor affecting the condition of comics is the fact that no one in the first three decades of publication thought much about preserving them, protecting them from the elements, or to even treat them with much respect. After all, it's this very fact that they were manufactured so cheaply, that allowed them to be sold for only a dime. This 10 cent cost is the very reason comics were within the budget range of the average American kid. If comics were not manufactured as a "deterioration time bomb," the hobby as we know it might not ever have gotten off the ground. And yet another piece of the comic book condition puzzle falls into place as we remember that they were not originally manufactured to last very long in the first place. And this leads us to the typical degradation scenario. These elements of "destruction" can be loosely described as follows:

First, the publisher selects the cheapest materials possible in order to maximize profit. Newsprint, a highly unstable mixture of wood pulp, acids and tannins, is chosen. This insures that the deterioration process will begin literally at the time of paper manufacture.

Second, the printer handles the job in the fastest and most economical way possible, caring about the handling of the product only to the minimum required for acceptance by the consumer. And in the first three decades of comic book production, consumers weren't all that picky.

After the printer's contribution to reduced condition it's time for the third villain to enter the picture, the bindery, where the folding, stapling, and trimming process is accomplished. It fulfills its obligatory role by mistrimming about 30% of the run, miscutting about 20% of the run, misfolding 15% of the run, off center stapling 25% of the run, and generally mistreating about 100% of the run. This mistreatment process ends up with the comic books being stacked on pallettes and tied with bundling wire, which of course contributes even more damage, especially to the books unlucky enough to end up in contact with the bundling wire, usually with the worst assaults at the top and bottom of the stacks.

Number four in our tragic play is the distributor. He is given the opportunity to treat the comics with disrespect by throwing (*and we do mean throwing*) the various individual store allotments into boxes for delivery.

When they finally arrive at the drug store or newsstand the comics are placed by the fifth condition villain onto shelves, or worse, into wire racks that bend, crease, and tear with every push and shove.

After all this, it's time for the ultimate preservation villain to enter the picture — none other than you and I in our youth. Imagine, if you will, a scene that has been repeated uncountable times across this fair continent. A ten-year- old rides up to the front door of the local pharmacy clad in T-shirt, blue jeans and sneakers. The youthful consumer enters the store and moves directly to the newsstand on the front wall, just inside the door. After an agonizing selection process, the young buyer chooses a copy of Flash Comics #105 (the first issue) which has already been reduced from its' original condition to (if conditions were fortunate) a very fine copy before the consumer even has an opportunity to purchase it. That's an important idea to remember and helps the collector to conceptualize that comics from 1933 through 1969 were rarely in mint condition, even fresh from the rack. The young purchaser plunks down his dime, neatly but firmly folds the comic book lengthwise, and places it snugly into a back pocket for the long bicycle ride home. Upon arriving there, this early "collector" then proceeds to treat the comic in the traditional way, that is, folding back and creasing each and every page, starting with the cover, in turn as it is read. This "fold 'em back as you go" style is ergonomically efficient as it allows the reader to hold the comic with one hand while maneuvering a rapidly melting popsicle with the other. At the conclusion of the reading process, the comic is tossed unceremoniously into a drawer, closet, or under the bed for temporary storage, to be retrieved later for rereading or possible trade with another thrifty comic fan in the neighborhood. The usual final merciful conclusion to this modern day preservation tragedy, is for a parent to trash the comic (now in well read very good or worse condition), use it for packing dishes, utilize the absorptive surface for a coaster, to replace the scrap doodling paper by the phone, helping the puppy train itself to be location specific, or finally to fulfill its ultimate destiny in the trash with the other magazines and newspapers. After all, it was only a cheaply mass produced, purposefully inexpensive, temporarily entertaining, comic book. Before its demise, this folded, split, torn, spine rolled, faded, stained, bent, creased, marked on, soiled, smeared, smudged, and ripped temporary piece of juvenile entertainment penetrated the psyche of its reader so deeply and completely, that it, and the stories it contained, became a permanent part of the happy memories that will forever be nostalgically recalled by its owner. Thus, we can understand two universals that are true in the field of comic book collecting. First, that the chances for pre-1970 comic books and some may argue any era of comic books to be in high grade are actually extremely low. This means that the number of copies of any given issue in high grade are significantly lower than the number of copies in middle and lower grades. And second, that people who collect these quasi-antique newsprint gems want them to be as identical as possible to their original manufactured condition for the most basic of reasons—esthetics. Once one realizes that (a) high grade copies are truly scarce items, (b) most collectors appreciate this fact, and (c) most collectors prefer higher grade copies, then one can see how the old story of supply and demand applies. Thus knowing how to grade comics is an important and essential skill for any one who fancies himself to be a comic book collector. Knowing how to grade is important if you are selling, if you are trading and especially if you are buying. Without the knowledge of grading, one does not have all the tools required for estimating value. Without insight into value determination, one may become a hapless victim of the market.

THE EVOLUTION OF COMIC BOOK GRADING

In order to understand the present system of comic book grading, it is important to understand the evolution of grading. Before the hobby of comic book collecting gained national attention during the early sixties, two other collectibles dominated America: coins and stamps. If one were to be perfectly logical, one might surmise that since stamps are made of paper, their grading system would be the most appropriate to apply to comics. More logical maybe, but many early comic book collectors had backgrounds as coin collectors. Thus the grading system for coins was adapted to the realm of comic books and for better or worse that system provided the fundamental terminology for the evaluation of condition used by collectors to this very day.

If we look back at the first half of the 20th century, the research shows a strong parallel between the development of the grading system for comics and the development of the grading system for coins. But in both cases, these systems have evolved to meet the needs of hobbyists whose ever increasing levels of sophistication require it.

To understand this increased need for evaluation accuracy we may note the parallel to our educational evaluation system. When one attends a traditional nursery school, two grades are sufficient to describe behavior:

S (Satisfactory)
U (Unsatisfactory)

Then in kindergarten and early primary school, the evaluation system is expanded from a 2 point system to a 3 point system:

+ (Above Average)
(Average)
- (Below Average)

By elementary school, a 5 point system known to many across the country is in place:

A (Excellent)
B (Above Average)
C (Average)
D (Below Average)
F (Failing)

In many schools grades 7 through 12 expand this to a 12 point system for even greater evaluative specificity:

A (Excellent)
A- (Excellent Minus)
B+ (Above Average Plus)
B (Above Average)
B- (Above Average Minus)
C+ (Average Plus)
C (Average)
C- (Average Minus)
D+ (Below Average Plus)
D (Below Average)
D- (Below Average Minus)
F (Failing)

Further expansion of academic evaluation is commonly used on testing and in some cases grades, that being the 100 point scale. Expanding from a 5 point scale (simple letter grades) to a 100 point scale (or percentage scale) allows a *20 fold increase* in the potential accuracy of the evaluation. Similarly, the grading of coins and comics can trace a similar evolution in their eventual expansion to a 100 point system.

In the 1932 edition of "The Star Rare Coin Encyclopedia" compiled and published by the Numismatic Company of Texas (B. Max Mehl, the foremost numismatics authority of his day) one cannot help but notice the obvious similarities between the generally accepted coin grading system in force in the 30s and the early comic book grading system informally "adopted" by early comic collectors a score of years later. The evolution of coin grading can be sampled by looking at the evaluation system in force for regular circulation coins in those early years.

Proof
Uncirculated (or "As Minted")
Fine
Good
Fair
Poor

As the need for more specific evaluation increased, the original "6 point" coin grading system expanded by adding grades in between existing grades. The first of these added grades were Very Fine and Extra Fine (or Extremely Fine), so that even greater descriptive accuracy could be achieved.

Proof
Uncirculated
Extra Fine (Extremely Fine)
Very Fine
Fine
Good
Fair
Poor

Eventually this was expanded to the 70 point scale now in use by coin collectors and coin grading services.

The comic book world also started with a "5 point scale" (excluding the term Proof) and by the mid to late 1950s had expanded to a 7 point scale. By the late to early 1960s the 8 point scale that most are familiar with was in common usage. Worthy of note were the mail order ads of those early years. In those primordial days of fandom, many collector/dealers resisted the use of grades at all and some even annotated their catalogs with the statements "Please do not make inquiries about condition," or "Inquires about condition will not be answered." This "no grading dogma" was eventually undermined by consumer pressure as a descriptive range was begrudgingly offered. These included such phrases as "All comics guaranteed to be in good or better condition" or a favorite non-descript description "All books are in Good to Mint condition unless otherwise noted."

By the mid to late 1950s, the basic five point scale grading system for comic books looked like this:

Mint
Fine
Good
Fair
Poor

It was expanded to a 7 point scale by adding the "in between grades" Very Good and Very Fine. This 7 point scale was in wide usage by fandom by the middle 1950s.

Mint
Very Fine
Fine
Very Good
Good
Fair
Poor

But this two point expansion did not satisfy some mail order sellers. After all, the word "mint" seemed to sell more books, so a number of them began to use the term "nearly mint" which was eventually foreshortened to "near mint," and was in common usage by the early 1960s. Thus the now familiar 8 point comic book evaluation system was born.

Mint
Near Mint
Very Fine
Fine
Very Good
Good
Fair
Poor

It's also worthy of note that the grades Very Good and Very Fine were originally considered "half grades" by comic book collectors, i.e. halfway between
the adjacent grades. When the grade Near Mint arrived on the scene as common usage, it caused a bit of confusion for early fandom, because it posed
this perplexing question: Is Very Fine 1/3 of the way to Mint and Near Mint
2/3 of the way to Mint? Or is Very Fine half way to Mint and Near Mint 3/4 of
the way? This question was never solved to general satisfaction until The
Overstreet Price Guide of 1989. At any rate, the original three "in between
grades" have been incorporated into the accepted grading scheme as "full
grades" and comprise the traditional 8 point comic book grading system familiar
to most modern collectors. The 100 point system utilized in this edition is the
next logical step towards greater evaluative accuracy.

98-100 (Mint)
90-97 (Near Mint)
75-89 (Very Fine)
55-74 (Fine)
35-54 (Very Good)
15-34 (Good)
5-14 (Fair)
1-4 (Poor)

Insight into the evolution of comic book grading can be of value to collectors
as they undertake the interesting task of learning about this most fascinating
topic. It is the sincerest hope of the authors that comic enthusiasts will consider all factors, both pragmatic and historical, as they expand their knowledge
and hone their grading skills.

USING THIS GRADING GUIDE

The General Grading Procedure:

Step 1:
Take the comic book you want to grade and lay it down on a flat clean surface. If it is in a plastic bag or mylar, carefully remove it. Make sure your examination area is well lighted, moisture free, and smokeless. Ensure that the
comic is not in direct sunlight or under unfiltered florescent light which may
generate ultra violet (the same bleaching agent as the sun).

Step 2:
While observing the cover, turn through the pictorial section of The Overstreet
Grading Guide and locate the illustrated examples which most closely match
the comic you are working with. After you have made the selection, turn forward and back to the nearest adjacent grades to double check your selection.

Step 3:
Look for and identify all the defects on the front and back covers, e.g.:
    (a) Condition of staples
    (b) Creases, fold, tears, stains, etc.
    (c) Ink reflectivity.

Step 4:
Note if any grade reduction is required for identified defects. Be very careful to note even small details as most collectors consider the cover the most important focus of evaluation.

Step 5:
Closely examine the spine. Note any defects which may affect the overall grade. Many collectors consider the condition of the spine one of the most important indicators of overall condition.

Step 6:
Look for and identify all the defects on the inside front cover and the inside back cover. Note if any grade reduction is required for these identified defects. Be sure to closely examine the area where the interior of the comic meets the cover. **IMPORTANT NOTE:** Do not open the cover of higher grade books more than approximately 45 degrees to avoid stressing the spine.

Step 7:
Turn to the center fold to make sure it has not been removed.

Step 8:
Check for and estimate whiteness level utilizing the OWL Card. A facsimile has been included in the color section of The Overstreet Grading Guide.

Step 9:
Note any structural or printing defects on interior pages. Pay careful attention to the presence of brittleness as evidenced by any chipping or flaking.

Step 10:
Review the defects which are acceptable and not acceptable for the grade you have chosen as the closest match.

OTHER CONSIDERATIONS:

Grading comic books is an art, not a science. In this light, do not expect to become expert at grading "overnight." Many collectors and dealers who have been at it for years still make errors occasionally. But take heart! With a little practice and application, the skill of grading comics can be mastered. If you keep a few things in mind, you can avoid some of the common pitfalls. Consider a few of the following strategies.

(a) It never hurts to get a reality check. If in doubt, get a second opinion from another collector or a "seasoned grading veteran" like a local mail order dealer or comic shop owner.

(b) Never grade a large quantity of comics all at one time. This can result in "grading burnout" which, of course, reduces the accuracy of your evaluation.

(c) If possible, keep a sample of each grade for reference. When the need arises, your samples will be ready for immediate comparison.

(d) Some of the more difficult differentiation occurs in the middle grades. Pay special attention to the lines of demarcation between the high end of fair and the lower end of good, the high end of good and the lower end of very good, and the high end of very good and the lower end of fine. Even long time collectors and dealers still have difficulty in these areas.

(e) Unless you know and trust the seller, always ask to inspect the inside of the comic before you buy it. This protects the seller and the buyer. A reasonable request might be to ask the seller to show you the inside of the comic. This courtesy permits the owner to do all the handling plus insures that the potential buyer has no liability if the book is accidentally damaged during handling. Above all, exercise politeness and appropriate human relations skills. Reputable dealers are (by definition) interested in making sure you are a happy buyer.

(f) No matter how specific the grading criteria, there will always be differences of opinion. A reasonable person will always respect a possible difference in interpretation. If in doubt, refer to and discuss the grading criteria and defects section in this publication. Whether buying, trading, or selling, one always has the option of declining the transaction before it is consummated.

(g) Comic books published before 1970 are scarce items in high grade. Many of the comics published before 1960 do not exist in mint condition and in many cases probably do not exist even in near mint, yet enthusiasts newly arrived to comic book collecting erroneously harbor the expectation that these books will eventually become available in these grades. This expectation will nearly always be doomed to disappointment. Long time collectors will quickly confirm this as they point out certain issues with the familiar phrase "I'm lucky to find a copy at all, much less in high grade."

HOW TO DESCRIBE COMIC BOOK CONDITION

(Mail Order Nomenclature or Advertising Nomenclature)
Below are a few general guidelines that can be effectively utilized when offering comic books for sale via mail order. These are by no means rigid, but are offered as a model that is in general acceptance at this writing. When advertising comic books through the mail, it is important to:

(a) Use a consistent format that both conserves valuable advertising space, yet gives complete information to the potential buyer. In general, it is always better to give too much information than not enough. An informed buyer has a much greater chance of being a happy buyer.

(b) Strive hard to grade accurately.

These two simple guidelines can save you work, time and money, and increase the potential for your mail order dealings to be not only successful, but enjoyable as well. These guidelines can also be applied when offering material for trade as well as for sale.

TRADITIONAL METHOD

List relevant information about each individual comic in the following order:

1. TITLE. e.g. Superman, Batman, Fantastic four, Adventures Into The Unknown, etc.
2. ISSUE NUMBER. e.g. #2, #256, V2#5, etc.
3. ABBREVIATION FOR THE OVERALL GRADE. e.g. PR, FR, GD, VG, FN, VF, NM, or MT.
4. ADDITIONAL PARENTHETICAL INFORMATION ABOUT CONDITION. e.g. interior grade, location, size, and severity of defects, restoration information if applicable, other grading notes.
5. ADDITIONAL PARENTHETICAL INFORMATION OTHER THAN CONDITION. e.g. pedigree, early or first appearances, origins, classic covers,

etc.

6. PRICE. e.g. $12, $150 or $27.50 ea.

General Examples:

Aquaman #1 fn $80.00

All Star #3 vg + (small chip out lower left, minor color touch urfc, great cover gloss, first JSA, scarce) $2300.00

Fantastic Four #1 fr (severe water damage to cover, small piece out llfc, inside fn, white pages, an excellent research copy) $150.00

Amazing Mystery Funnies V2#7 vf + (beautiful mile high copy, completely unrestored, rare, intro Fantom Of The Fair, would be nm except for ½'' tear lrbc, fantastic original gloss, white pages) $3900.00

NEW METHOD

Use **The Comic Book Grading Card (One/Owl)** (see color section, first page). The **ONE** side of the card may be used to convert traditional grades to the new numerical grades. The **OWL** side will aid you in determining the whiteness level of your comic books. Cards will be available through all regular channels or may be purchased direct from the publisher. **Note:** The **ONE/OWL** card was created as a quick reference tool for determining a more precise and total description of a comic book's condition. As with the Traditional Method, list relevant information about each individual comic in the following order:

1. TITLE. e.g. Superman, Batman, Fantastic Four, Adventures Into the Unknown, etc.

2. ISSUE NUMBER e.g. #2, #256, V2#5, etc.

3. Consult the **ONE/OWL** comic book grading card and LIST GRADE FOLLOWED BY **ONE** VALUE & **OWL** VALUE SEPARATED BY ''/''. e.g. FN60/5.

4. ADDITIONAL PARENTHETICAL INFORMATION ABOUT CONDI- TION. e.g. interior grade, whiteness value, location, size, and severity of defects, restoration information if applicable, other grading notes.

5. ADDITIONAL PARENTHETICAL INFORMATION OTHER THAN CON- ITION. e.g. pedigree, early or first appearances, origins, classic covers, etc.

6. PRICE. e.g. $12, $150 or $27.50 ea.

General Examples

Aquaman #1 FN65/6 . . . . $80.00

All Star #3 VG50/5 (small chip out lower left, minor color touch urfc, great ink reflectivity, first JSA, scarce) $2300.00

Fantastic Four #1 FR10/5 (severe water damage to cover, small piece out llfc, an excellent research copy) $150.00

Amazing Mystery Funnies V2#7 VF85/8 (beautiful mile high copy, completely unrestored, rare, intro Fantom Of The Fair, ½'' tear lrbc, fantastic original ink reflectivity $3900.00

DIAGRAM OF A COMIC BOOK

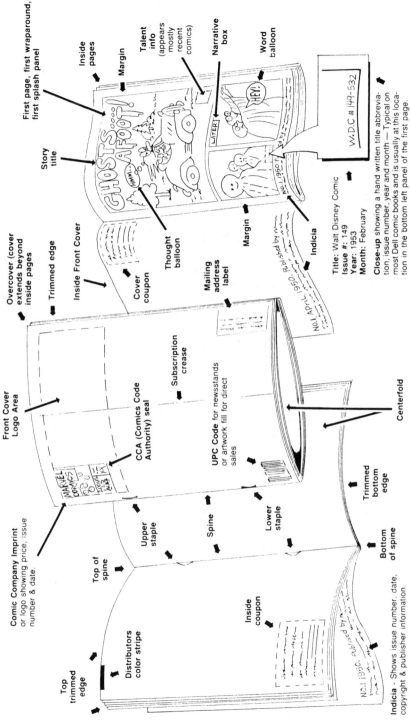

First page, first wraparound, first splash panel

Inside pages

Margin

Talent info (appears mostly recent comics)

Narrative box

Word balloon

Story title

Thought balloon

Margin

Indicia

Overcover (cover extends beyond inside pages)

Trimmed edge

Inside Front Cover

Cover coupon

Mailing address label

Title: Walt Disney Comic
Issue #: 149
Year: 1953
Month: February

Close-up showing a hand written title abbreviation, issue number, year and month — Typical on most Dell comic books and is usually at this location in the bottom left panel of the first page.

Front Cover Logo Area

Subscription crease

CCA (Comics Code Authority) seal

UPC Code for newsstands or artwork fill for direct sales

Centerfold

Comic Company Imprint or logo showing price, issue number & date.

Top of spine

Upper staple

Spine

Lower staple

Bottom of spine

Trimmed bottom edge

Top trimmed edge

Distributors color stripe

Inside coupon

Indicia - Shows issue number, date, copyright & publisher information.

RESTORATION NOTES

by

Susan Cicconi

(Authors Note: Susan Cicconi, "Conservator of Ephemera," is nationally recognized as a leading expert on the art and science of comic book conservation and restoration. She is owner and sole operator of **The Restoration Lab** *located in Boston, Massachusetts.)*

The vast majority of comic books were printed on highly acidic newsprint (the cheapest grade of paper available) and, for the most part, were not intended to be permanently preserved. Who could have imagined that comic books bought at the newsstand for 10¢ would eventually command such incredible prices (depending on condition and rarity) some fifty years later? The need for professional conservation is the inevitable result of increased cultural appreciation for "old comic books," as well as high prices. Most comic books submitted for restoration are generally soiled and torn with the often well-intentioned (but regrettably naive) attempt at repair using various mending glues and adhesive tapes. In most cases, the extent to which some books have been treated has rendered these attempted repairs irreversible! Since my role as paper conservator is, in part, educational, the following checklist may help collectors *identify* these unskilled attempts at restoration. With a little practice, collectors can learn to readily recognize these.

1. COLOR TOUCH-UP (COLOR TOUCH)

(a) Ball point pen — Shiny when viewed at a raking light, blue and black. (b) Felt-tip pen — Bleed through to inside of cover, especially reds, blues, greens, purples, and black. (c) Water color — Bleed through when incorrectly applied; opaque and pasty when incorrectly applied.

Most likely areas for color touch-up: (a) Exterior of front and back covers. (b) Exterior of spine at stress marks, hairline creases, and along black lines. (c) Corner creases and folds.

Note: When examining for Color Touch-Up, it is necessary to gently look along the inside of the spine for bleed-through. Special care should be exercised during the examination as improper handling may result in damage to the comic book.

Note: **NEVER** *use ball point pen or felt tip pen for color touch for any reason.*

2. MENDING PAPERS

(a) Look for mending at areas of support including staple holes, along spine, and at edge tears. Open the cover to expose the inside of the spine at staple holes. (b) Check both sides of centerfold at staple holes for any mended tears as these tears can be very small.

Note: When examining for mending papers, it is necessary to gently look along the inside of the spine for bleed-through. Special care should be exercised during the examination as improper handling may result in damage to the comic book.

3. MISSING PIECE REPLACEMENT

The most likely areas for Missing Piece Replacement are along spine, corners, and margins ("Marvel Chipping"). Carefully hold comic book up to the light, open front and back covers (one at a time) so that each half can be viewed in front of the light.

4. COVER RE-GLOSSING

If cover looks excessively glossy and is heavier and thicker to the touch, chances are it has been sprayed with a fixative which will result in irreversible damage.

5. MECHANICAL OR "DRY" CLEANING

Difficult to detect unless there are noticeable streaks and spots where *erasures* have been incorrectly used.

*Note: DO NOT CONFUSE this with traditional laundry dry cleaning which uses the solvent Carbon Tetrachloride. This solvent is **extremely** toxic and **extremely** flammable and should never be used in a poorly ventilated area and/or near open flame. Never use this solvent on paper for any reason.*

6. CHEMICAL OR "SOLVENT" CLEANING

When correctly performed, impossible to detect. When incorrectly performed, covers will retain the transfer stain and/or a possible residual chemical odor.

7. AQUEOUS OR "WATER" CLEANING

If incorrectly treated, covers and interior pages will feel flimsy and light and will warp and cockle. There is also the possibility of color fading.

8. TAPE REMOVAL

Look for residual yellow or brown stains that are rectangular in shape. Locations will vary throughout cover and interior, with more emphasis on support areas (spine, corners, centerfold).

9. STAPLE REPLACEMENT

This is a difficult detection. Staples should be viewed from the inside, that is, at the centerfold page. Look to see that the points of the staple which meet are tight and pronounced. Prongs of staple should line up perfectly to any indents in the paper. It is almost impossible to replace "original" staples in their precise location.

10. SPINE ROLL REMOVAL

When correctly done it is impossible to detect. When incorrectly performed — you'll still see the spine roll.

11. DEACIDIFICATION

This process requires professional expertise. Improper application can result in *irreversible damage.* Covers which have been incorrectly sprayed can result in color flaking, ink bleeding, and "cockling." Interiors may warp and/or severely darken.

12. BLEACHING

When incorrectly treated, covers and interiors will be excessively white, gritty with washed out or faded colors. A residual foreign odor is sometimes present.

Before restoration: *All Star Comics* #3, 1940. © DC Comics, Inc. Note heavy tape and soiling along spine.

After restoration: *All Star Comics* #3, 1940. © DC Comics, Inc.

Before restoration: *Marvel Comics* #1, 1939. © Marvel Ent. Group. Note front and back cover are completely separated; front cover is torn in two; chunks are missing from back cover.

After restoration: *Marvel Comics* #1, 1939. © Marvel Ent. Group.

13. TRIMMING

Probably the most difficult detection. This is most visible on Silver Age books — DC, Marvel, EC. Most of these books have a very slight overhang or "overcover" (1/16") at the top and bottom margin of front and back covers. Because of improper storage or handling, the cover will crease at the top and eventually tiny tears will form. Attempts have been made to alter the book, irreversibly, by trimming the excess margin flush with the interior pages. Trimming is often suspected if the interior pages are flush on the top and bottom of the margin, *unless* it is a book of extremely high grade with no other evidence of repair. Interior pages have also been found to be trimmed. Snags in the paper are visible and the trimmed edges are usually slightly lighter in color than the rest of the book.

Before restoration: *Captain America Comics* #1, 1941. © Marvel Ent. Group. Note soiled spine area with tears.

After restoration: *Captain America* #1, 1941. © Marvel Ent. Group.

Professional Comic Book Conservation.

The conservation of comic books fulfill two primary functions: Restoration *and* preservation. Professional restoration methods may include a variety of techniques, such as general non-abrasive cleaning, tape and stain removal, paper reinforcement/replacement, and color inpainting. Professional restoration is a very meticulous process which emphasizes structural as well as esthetic enhancement. The materials used must be of the highest quality. The craftsmanship must always strive to maintain the highest standard of excellence and professionalism.

The key word is *professional*. Only *professional* restoration can increase the value of comic books. Take, as an example, a 1940 VG copy of a *Batman #1*. It is worn and torn with a spine that is frayed and splitting. The cover is slightly soiled and discolored with creases and stress marks. It has a severe spine roll. This comic appears almost "lifeless." Upon closer examination, the cover has no pieces missing, colors are still vivid and not faded. There is no evidence of previous restoration, tapes, or other adhesives. The interior pages are supple and tanning and the staples are clean and tight. This copy of *Batman #1* is an optimal candidate for restoration. Through a series of very careful and meti-

Before and after: *Captain America* #1, 1941. © Marvel Ent. Group. Note restoration to pieces missing from the left edge.

culous procedures (cleaning, paper reinforcement, spine repair, color inpainting, pressing, and possibly deacidification) this *Batman #1* will now have a Very Fine appearance and is preserved for many years to come. The comic book is structurally sound and tight, pages will remain supple, colors are cleaner and therefore brighter — in short, this *Batman #1* lives once again!

These basic but often painstaking techniques of restoration can be applied to most **Golden Age** books. It has been my experience that early *Detective, Batman, Action* and *Superman* (DC Publications) are prime candidates for restoration because of paper malleability and responsiveness. There are exceptions, however, since particular compositions of inks, fiber furnish and fiber sizes, varied from one publisher to another. *Marvel Mystery* and *Captain America* (Timely Publications), for example, will react differently to certain procedures, (not necessarily adversely) but the paper stock of these comics is not as cooperative.

The most difficult books to restore are the **Silver Age** titles such as *Amazing Spider-Man, Incredible Hulk, Fantastic Four, X-Men, Avengers*, etc. (Marvel

Before and after restoration: *Detective Comics* #18, 1938. © DC Comics, Inc. Note large scraped area in logo.

Publications). The paper composition of these books differs greatly from Golden Age comics with respect to size, weight, colors and inks. Because of these complex properties, it is necessary to carefully choose between structural and esthetic repair. Experience has shown that it is best to take care of defects that affect the book structurally, such as tears, loose or rusted staples, spine rolls, creases and folds. A simple solvent wash (as opposed to a water wash) will greatly improve the book visually be removing the ''yellowing'' particularly present in these early Marvel titles. This is sometimes referred to as a transfer stain since ink particles have migrated to the inside covers from the first and last pages. This is not to be confused with ''browning'' which is an actual acid transference of the interior pages onto the cover, breaking down the cellulose paper fibers and causing them to age and discolor. This ''yellowing'' can be completely removed with no adverse effects to dimensions (size), gloss (ink reflectivity) or color. The cover is cleaner, whiter and colors are brighter.

The comics of Disney and EC Publications fall in between Golden Age and Silver Age with regard to restoration potential. Disney is closer to Golden Age with its large format, 16 folios, heavier stock paper. Structural and esthetic repair are performed with excellent results. EC Comics resemble those of early Marvel titles where the emphasis is more on structural repair. The covers and interior pages of numerous EC Comics show sign of advanced aging and discoloration (browning). Many of these books will benefit from deacidification. This must be done while the pages are still flexible.

Annuals and other ''square-bound'' (perfect bound) comics such as *World's Fair,* and early *World's Finest* are in a special class by themselves. These books generally contain several pages held tightly with large heavy staples and the covers (composed of a thick pulpy stock) are glued directly onto the spine of the interior pages with very strong adhesive. It is extremely difficult to treat these covers unless they are loose, frayed and splitting away from the interior. If possible, mechanical separation would be required for restoration. If the cover is not loose yet needs cleaning, pressing, and possible tear reinforcement (which

Before restoration: *Showcase* #4, 1956. © DC Comics, Inc. Note damage along spine and cover corners.

After restoration: *Showcase* #4, 1956. © DC Comics, Inc.

is very often the case), then the process can only be accomplished within certain limitations.

Having discussed some of the best candidates for restoration, it is also important to recognize **when NOT to restore a comic book.** On occasion rare books of high grade are submitted for restoration because the cover is missing a miniscule piece at the margin or there is a slight pencil marking or hairline crease with color loss. Other than these minor defects, the books were beautiful copies, sound and flat, clean with supple pages, tight staples, etc. It is my strong feeling and the consensus of most seasoned collectors that the appropriate course is to leave these books in their natural, unrestored state. Repairing any of these tiny defects is NOT true restoration.

There are two general guidelines used to determine if a comic book is a candidate for restoration:

A) Items should be worth at least $150 — $200 in their present condition.

With rates exceeding $60 per hour for a simple cleaning and pressing it is not cost effective to request a full structural and esthetic enhancement on an item of lesser value unless unique conditions exist.

B) Always consider structural repair *before* esthetic repair.

Tear and spine reinforcement, cleaning or replacing rusted staples, spine roll removal, general cleaning and pressing of creases and folds, solvent wash, can all greatly contribute to the structural support of the book while also enhancing its visual impact.

Additionally, if budget permits, missing piece replacement at corners and at the top and bottom of the spine, followed by color inpainting, will ultimately complete and enhance the book's esthetic impact. (There is nothing wrong with color inpainting provided it is applied onto the filled area and not used as a measure to mask stains and discolorations.)

All in all, it is important to consider the proper techniques necessary to insure that comic books retain their suppleness, cover lustre, and page whiteness. Simple measures such as proper storage in a heat, light and humidity controlled environment, the use of archival preservation supplies, and, when necessary, deacidification of interior pages. Restoration, when done professionally, can greatly enhance the longevity of these fragile, valuable, and rare paper treasures.

—Susan Cicconi, 1992

MARK WILSON

ON

COMIC BOOK RESTORATION

(Author's Note: Mark Wilson has pioneered many new and innovative comic book restoration techniques and is a nationally known expert in the fields of paper chemistry and paper aging. The Overstreet Comic Book Grading Guide interviewed Mark at his home in Washington state. A condensed version of his remarks follows.)

Why are comic books restored?

In my experience, there seem to be three main reasons. First and foremost, to improve the appearance of the comic for the collector. Second, often to literally save the book from complete deterioration. And third is for profit. This last motivation may sound a bit greedy, but it is simply another way to earn a living. To begrudge an individual making money in this area would be the same as telling a person not to invest in comic books with an eye for profit.

What do you feel is the biggest misconception about comic book restoration?

That it's bad. People follow the crowd. For the last three years people have been afraid of restoration because some of the publicity has been negative.

Would you discuss amateur versus professional restoration?

The old saying "You get what you pay for" fits this topic well. You will actually pay a little more for a professional to work on your comic books, but, in the long run, it is always the most cost effective way to go. You are paying for, in many cases, thousands of hours of research when you commission a trained professional to work on your book. The results will not only look better, but you can be assured that the work will be in accordance with archival quality standards. After viewing hundreds of amateurly restored books over the years, I have come to the conclusion that it would be better to leave a book in its unrestored state rather than have a "friend" fix it. One must understand that restoration is both art and science. Some unenlightened would-be restorers tend to forget the scientific aspects and attempt to "paint" their way out of most every problem. Coloring is really one of the final steps of the process.

What is meant by the "Doctrine Of Reversibility?"

One of the most critical points in performing restoration is reversibility. For example, all adhesives used must have the ability to be removed at a later date. In other words, all sealed tears can be unsealed by an expert in the future, if required. All pieces added and all rice paper reinforcement can be removed. All sizing added can be removed. The only exception to this rule would be in the area of color touch. Unlike the above, proper color touch should be permanent, which is why it is so important that it be perfect the first time. Once applied, there is no going back.

What do professionals use for color touch?

Two of the most popular choices among professional restorers are acrylics and printers ink. Both are, for the most part, permanent. Acrylic is water base prior to application but is no longer water soluble after it dries. Printers ink is oil based. It is solvent soluble, but so are all inks used on a comic book. All other media either crack, chip, have poor flexibility or, being water soluble, come off in your hands with mild perspiration. The consideration of flexibility is important. Unlike restoring paintings and other forms of art, comic books consist of movable pages which are bent back and forth when a book is read. Glues, fixatives and color touch materials have to be able to move without chipping or breaking.

Modern collectors often discuss the acidity of pH of the comic book pages. Could you explain what is meant by pH? It's a fairly simple concept. It's a system of expressing acidity or alkalinity that was invented by Dr. Sorensen in 1909. Before then there was no exact way for one chemist to express the degree of acidity or alkalinity of a solution to another chemist. Water, which is pure (HOH) contains hydrogen (H) and oxygen (O). The water molecule splits into hydrogen ions (H) and hydroxyl ions (OH). Every H ion must have a corresponding OH ion in absolutely pure (and neutral) water so that the two kinds of ions are equal in number. Pure water is perfectly neutral; it is neither acid nor alkaline. The definition of a neutral solution is one where the H and OH ions are present in exactly equal amounts. H ions produce acidity, OH ions produce alkalinity. As equal numbers of each balance one another, the liquid is neither acid nor alkaline.

An acid occurs when this balance becomes unequal and more hydrogen ions exist than hydroxyl ions. The opposite condition is alkaline, that is, more hydroxyl ions and less hydrogen ions. Thus when one kind of ion increases, the other decreases a corresponding proportion. If the H ions are increased 10 times, the OH ions are decreased to 1/10, so what was 10 and 10 in a neutral solution may become 100 and 1. In a perfectly neutral solution the concentration of acid and alkali are exactly equal; and this is expressed as a "pH 7.0."

If we increase the hydroxyl ion by 10 times (above pH 7.0) by adding an alkali, the expressed pH value is increased by 1.0 and written pH 8.0. A mental chart expressing the pH scale can help one visualize the relationship of the common pH values and what they actually mean. It's really very easy to learn. Start with the alkaline side, that is a pH above 7.0.

pH 7.0 is neutral.
pH 8.0 represents 10 times the concentration of hydroxyl ions contained in a neutral solution.
pH 9.0 represents 100 times the concentration of hydroxyl ions contained in a neutral solution.
pH 10.0 represents 1,000 times the concentration of hydroxyl ions contained in a neutral solution.
pH 11.0 represents 10,000 times the concentration of hydroxyl ions contained in a neutral solution.
pH 12.0 represents 100,000 times the concentration of hydroxyl ions in a neutral solution.
pH 13.0 represents 1,000,000 times the concentration of hydroxyl ions contained in a neutral solution.

Below pH 7.0 is the acid side. It goes:

pH 7.0 is neutral.
pH 6.0 represents 10 times the concentration of hydrogen ions contained in a neutral solution.
pH 5.0 represents 100 times the concentration of hydrogen ions contained in a neutral solution.
pH 4.0 represents 1,000 times the concentration of hydrogen ions contained in a neutral solution.
pH 3.0 represents 10,000 times the concentration of hydrogen ions contained in a neutral solution.
pH 2.0 represents 100,000 times the concentration of hydrogen ions contained in a neutral solution.
pH 1.0 represents 1,000,000 times the concentration of hydrogen ions contained in a neutral solution.

That's basically it in simple terms.

Many collectors are considering having their comic books deacidified. What's your opinion of deacidification?

The Declaration of Independence is sealed in an inert gas and locked away in a dark area for preservation. If deacidification is the perfected process everyone says it is then why don't they deacidify this document? Well, the answer is, the jury is still out on this issue and the experts do not want to gamble on unperfected technology and take a chance that might permanently damage this valuable document. All they have done is to seal it off from contact with the air in order to slow the aging process.

An example of "jumping the gun" on this unperfected technology was the polymer spray that was originally invented in Russia in the 1960s and later developed in the States for libraries. It was sprayed on newspapers to slow yellowing and aging. At first it seemed to preserve quite nicely, but in a few years it yellowed up badly and they lost all the paper that they tried to preserve. Not only that but the polymer bonded with the paper fibers and was irreversible. Also, in the past, many have used VPD paper to deacidify, which caused problems. Other solutions and sprays haven't worked well either.

Today, deacidification is still a big question mark in my mind. I personally wouldn't be in such a hurry to have comic books deacidified. Comics right off the press were already at a pH of 4.5 to 4.9 or at the best 5.0. And many of these that were stored under the right conditions are still white and fresh like new. i.e. take the Edgar Church copies as an example. Unless the comic is in really dire straits, I'd wait a bit until the technology is perfected.

Another point. Because groundwood pulp (from which newsprint is made) has some acid content to begin with, people think that deacidification (the addition of alkaline buffers) will neutralize the acid and therefore make the books last longer. Actually, there is no conclusive proof in my mind that deacidification is absolutely necessary to prolong the life of paper.

My overall position is that any time the restoration of a book requires disassembly and deacidification, it should be done by a professional. However, in my opinion, a blanket statement saying one should take all his comic books and deacidify them is not cost effective, is probably not even necessary, and could be ill-advised with the present technology. As you can see, I have real questions about deacidification. When future technology proves that deacidification is necessary and can be done in a safe manner, then I would recommend it to be done.

On the other hand, original art which is framed and exposed to the atmosphere and light should probably be deacidified. There are many facets one must consider when delving into this very complex question.

How should comic books be stored?

Proper storage methods is the single most important way to prolong the life of your comic books. Current, existing comic books, even those with brown pages, will probably last for 100 to several hundreds of years, if stored properly. To illustrate this point, I've found literally hundreds and hundreds of examples of groundwood pulp from 1860 through the 1920s, '30s, and '40s with pure white pages! It was at a library in San Francisco and they were stored in a cool, dark, dry basement. No other storage methods were used. The virgin white newsprint was preserved by nothing more than a good storage environment. I'm a strong advocate of the fact that being educated about proper storage and handling methods is by far the most important preservation technique. In fact, that's the most important lesson. **Proper storage conditions are:** Cool, dry, dark, shielded from rodent, insect, and fungus attack (eliminate moisture and you eliminate fungus). Relative humidity can be from 40 to 75 per cent.

Avoid heat or high humidity with heat and ultra violet light. Use incandescent, not florescent light. Staples are metal and moisture will condense on them. To keep staples from rusting the book should be wrapped in an absorbent, non-acid material.

What do you think is the best comic book storage product?

Mylar™ is the best product presently being produced for this purpose. And it is actually the most cost effective at this time. Interestingly, a lot of people don't realize that Mylar™ sleeves do contain some plastisizers. In order for them to be heat sealed and be flexible, they must introduce some plasticizers. In spite of this, it is still by far the best thing on the market for comic book storage at this time. One interesting note is that Mylar™ has a melting point well below the flash point of paper. This means that a comic book stored in Mylar™ will be laminated by this melting plastic before it will itself burst into flames.

Which type of comic book damage is the most difficult to repair?

Smoke damage is the most difficult damage to repair. Without a doubt.

What is sizing?

Sizing is a coating put on newsprint to keep the ink from bleeding (or diffusing) into the paper fibers. Here's a bit of a history lesson. The first material that was written on was animal skin. It could be written on with berry juice and other organic dyes because it did not absorb into them readily and therefore there was no bleeding. (An example of bleeding is like when you touch a felt tip pen or fountain pen to facial tissue.) The next step was parchment. It contains heavy oils which precludes absorption in the same way. Sizing accomplishes the same thing for wood pulp based paper, that is to preclude absorption. Sizing was first derived in the 1400s from rendering animals into animal-based gelatin sizing. Then they switched to Alum/Rosin sizing which is like distilled tree sap. That has a pH of about 4.0 to 4.5. All books that I know of use A/R sizing from about 1890 through the late 1940s or early 1950s. They would also add in some Aluminum Sulfate which would help speed up the sizing application by reducing drying time and further reduce ink absorption. In a way, sizing is simply an attempt to turn woodpulp into parchment! (As an aside, this explains why improperly applied color touch is usually extremely easy to spot, because at areas of increased wear, paper fibers are broken and sizing is worn off. This causes the applied color to bleed. Bare paper fibers are exposed at creases because of the break down of the sizing.) Re-sizing is simply the re-application of this coating as a restoration process.

Thank you, Mark, for your excellent information.

It was my pleasure. I appreciate the opportunity to share some of my ideas and perspectives on this intriguing topic. I wish all your readers happy collecting!

Mylar is a trademark of the Dupont Company.

A WORD ABOUT MAIL ORDER

The vast majority of all mail order comic book dealers are honest and fair. They commonly keep in stock literally thousands of comics, all of which must be graded before they are advertised for sale. As you can imagine, the logistics of such an endeavor is no simple task. On occasion, a comic gets through that may have been inadvertently overgraded or undergraded. If you by chance receive a book through the mail that you feel does not meet its advertised grade, don't panic. Simply call or write the dealer and discuss calmly the reasons for your opinion. The vast majority of dealers will gladly refund your money if you return the book in the original condition sent within a reasonable amount of time, even if they don't agree with your grading evaluation.

Many seasoned collectors successfully acquire comics by mail by following a few other simple steps. Before ordering, you may want to consider the following suggestions:

a) Call and ask the dealers to supply a few references. Reputable dealers will be happy to do it. They hope you will eventually become a reference as well.

b) Order a few things to see if you like their pricing and grading system. These tests are safely done with lower value orders. After you are satisfied with your initial "test" orders you may feel more comfortable spending larger amounts of money.

c) Continue to talk with the dealers by telephone occasionally. This is a great way to get to know them and for them to get to know you. Telephone calls are an excellent investment and can eliminate many unnecessary misunderstandings.

d) Write your orders clearly and legibly! Include all the information needed to successfully fill your order. Follow the ordering instructions listed by the dealer. Always write out your complete name and address on your order, as sometimes checks and envelopes may become separated from letters.

e) Always include a telephone number with your correspondence so that the dealer may contact you if questions arise or there is a problem with your order.

f) Understand that checks are slower to process than money orders or cashier's checks. Knowing this, the best approach seems to be to make a few orders using checks, since they provide an excellent record of the transaction, even though your order will take a little longer. After you become comfortable with the mail order dealer and feel you have a good business relationship, your order can be expedited with the use of either cashier's checks or money orders.

g) Be as courteous and reasonable with the dealers as you would like them to be courteous and reasonable with you. Many a good mail order relationship has been spoiled because individuals did not practice even the most basic human relations skills.

h) If you return books, be able to prove it. This is accomplished via postal receipts and insurance slips. Dealers and customers are not responsible for items until they sign for them. Never chance it! Always make sure there is some sort of official record proving the comics were returned, even for an inexpensive order. Retain all related documentation for at least one full year after the transaction. Good customers keep good records!

i) If nothing seems to work to ameliorate a problem, contact the publication, periodical, or newspaper that carried the dealer's advertisement. Sometimes they can intercede on your behalf. It is important to do this in writing! List the FACTS about the transaction in question without being dramatic or sensational. Call afterwards to make sure your letter was received. Inform the dealer about your letter or, better yet, send him/ her a copy of the letter. Make the goal of your letter and your efforts resolving the problem, not hurting reputations or feelings. Telephone calls won't work all by themselves. Put your concern or complaint in writing.

The authors have been successfully ordering by mail since the 1950s, with a high level of satisfaction. Along with comic book conventions and shops, mail order continues to be a key source for scarce material as well as an expedient, efficient, and cost effective method for collectors from all over the world to buy, sell, and trade comic books.

GRADE: MINT
Abbreviated Notation: MT

Overstreet **N**umerical **E**quivalent (**ONE**) range: **100-98**
(**Highest** possible MT grade = 100, **Mid**-grade = 99, **Lowest** possible MT grade = 98)

GRADE DESCRIPTION:
Near perfect in every way. Only the most subtle printing or bindery defects allowed. Cover is flat with no surface wear. Cover inks are bright with high reflectivity and minimal fading. Corners are cut square and sharp. Small, light pencilled, stamped or inked arrival dates are acceptible as long as they are in an unobtrusive or aesthetical location. Staples must be original and are generally centered and clean with no rust. Books signed on the inside do not detract from this grade. Cover is well centered and firmly secured to interior pages. Paper is supple and like new. Spine is tight and flat.

CHECKLIST FOR THE GRADE MINT:

- Near perfect in every way.
- No printing defects.
- No bindery defects.
- Cover is flat with no surface wear.
- Cover is bright.
- Cover is generally well centered.
- Staples are clean with no rust.
- Spine is flat and tight (no spine roll).
- Minute color fading is acceptable.
- No soiling, staining, or other discoloration.
- No hint of acidity in the odor of the newsprint.
- The overall look of a Mint condition comic book is "As if it was just purchased from the newsstand."

Note: Comic books published before 1970 in Mint condition are extremely scarce. This grade is one of the least understood and most abused of all comic book grades.

COLLECTOR ALERT: Collectors should thoroughly examine any book touted to be in this grade. Further, they should be carefully scrutinized for restoration.

COLLECTOR ALERT: Expensive/key comic books listed as being in "high grade" often have some restoration. In most cases restoration performed on otherwise mint books will reduce the grade. A near mint comic book **cannot** be transformed into a mint comic book through restoration.

GRADE: **MINT** (ONE - **100**)

Example: Front cover of *March Of Comics* #42, 1949. © Warner Bros.
Obvious defects: None.
Hidden defects: None.
OWL: 7.

All four corners
are sharp

Spine is tight
and flat

Staples are absent in
this binding process

A beautiful, flat, flawless copy

Note: This book has a newsprint cover and glued binding instead of staples. Because the cover is printed on newsprint stock the reflectivity is extremely low but does not affect the grade.

MINT (continued) - *March Of Comics*
Example: Front cover close ups.

No bindery defects

No soiling, staining or discoloration of any kind

Cover color is bright and well defined

No printing defects

Note: Comic books with newsprint (soft) covers are extremely rare in grades higher than **ONE** 90.

GRADE: **MINT** (ONE - **100**)

Example: Front cover of *Marge's Little Lulu* #15, 1949. © Marjorie H. Buell.
Obvious defects: None.
Hidden defects: None.
OWL: 7.

Spine is tight and flat.

Cover color is bright and well defined.

Tight spine, sharp corners, brilliant colors, and flat

All four corners are sharp

Note: This example is a perfect, flawless copy from the famous Western Printing Company file copy collection.

MINT (continued) - *Marge's Little Lulu*
Example: Front cover close ups.

No bindery defects

No printing defects

Flawless book - no defects.

GRADE: **MINT** (ONE - 100)

Example: Front cover of *Walt Disney's Donald Duck In Disneyland* #1, 1955. © The
Walt Disney Co.
Obvious defects: None.
Hidden defects: None.
OWL: 8.

A perfect, flawless book

All corners are sharp

Spine is perfect

Colors are brilliant

Note: This example is a "square bound" comic book and is from the famous Western
Printing Co. file copy collection. Dell square bounds notoriously occur in low grade.

MINT (continued) - *Walt Disney's Donald Duck In Disneyland*
Example: Front cover close ups.

Sharp corners

Sharp
corners

GRADE: **MINT** (ONE - **100**)

Example: Front cover of *Avengers* #11, 1963. © Marvel
Obvious defects: None.
Hidden defects: None.
OWL: 8.

Flawless book - no defects.

Note: This era of comic books often suffers from the defect called Marvel Chipping
(see glossary).

Flawless book - no defects.

GRADE: **MINT** (ONE - **99**)

Example: Front cover of *All Select* #2, 1943, © Marvel Comics.
Obvious defects: None.
Hidden defects: Printer smudge (see glossary) in margin of inside page which does not affect story.
OWL: 8.

Tiny color fleck

Colors are brilliant

Corners are sharp

Spine is tight and flat

Colors are brilliant

Cover is flat and clean

Note: This book is from the famous "San Francisco" collection of high quality books.

Mint (continued) - *All Select*
Example: Front cover close ups.

Tiny color
fleck

Note: This beautiful example is from the famous "San Francisco" collection.

All corners
are sharp

Staple is
off-center
but tight

Light, book-length
dust shadow

Note flat, clean and extra white
back cover

Note: The example above has only one staple, typical of many comic books of the World War II era and is not a defect.

GRADE: **MINT** (ONE - 99)

Example: Front cover of *Strange Adventures* #21, 1952. © DC Comics.
Obvious defects: None.
Hidden defects: None.
OWL: 9.

No printing
defects

Cover color is
bright and well
defined

Note transparent
cover (see glossary)

Off center
staples

Spine is tight
and flat

Flawless book except for
the bindery defect, type 1b

All four corners
are sharp

Note: This near perfect copy is from the "White Mountain" collection.

MINT (continued) - *Strange Adventures*
Example: Front cover close ups.

Flawless book except for
the bindery defect, type 1b

GRADE: **MINT** (ONE - 99)

Example: Front cover of *My Little Margie* #1, 1954. © Charlton Comics.
Obvious defects: None.
Hidden defects: None.
OWL: 7.

Note: This comic book has a double cover (see glossary). Although the double cover condition is technically a bindery defect, it actually enhances the collector value. Usually inside covers are in better condition. The condition of the outermost cover does not affect the overall grade if the inner cover(s) is of higher grade, as is usually the case. Description of books with multiple covers should include a grade for each cover.

Tiny corner nick

Printers color ink skip (see glossary)

Double cover

Tight spine

Sharp corners

MINT (continued) - *My Little Margie*
Example: First cover is open exposing the second cover.

Double cover

Indicia
(see glossary)

GRADE: **MINT** (ONE - 99)

Example: Front cover of *Western Tales Of Black Rider* #30, 1955. © Marvel Ent. Group.
Obvious defects: None.
Hidden defects: None.
OWL: 9. (Atlas western comics are very rare in this grade).

Sharp
edges

Tight
spine

Brilliant colors

Sharp corners

MINT (continued) - *Western Tales Of Black Rider*
Example: Front cover close ups.

Sharp corners

Tiny color fleck

GRADE: **MINT** (ONE - 99)

Example: Front cover of *Strange Tales* #93, 1962. © Marvel Comics.
Obvious defects: None.
Hidden defects: Maverick staple (see glossary).
OWL: 9.

Note: This excellent example is from the "White Mountain" collection.

Tiny inked date

Tight spine, sharp corners, brilliant colors, and flat

Note: The small date written in ink immediately under issue number does not detract from the overall beauty of this "prehero" Marvel comic book (see glossary). Many other Marvel books from this era are plagued with Marvel chipping (see glossary).

GRADE: **MINT** (ONE - 99)

Example: Front cover of *The Atom* #7, 1963. © DC Comics.
Obvious defects: None.
Hidden defects: None.
OWL: 8.

Exceptional quality and color intensity.

Spine is tight

No printing
defects

All four corners
are sharp

MINT (continued) - *The Atom*
Example: Front cover close ups.

Absolutely no surface soiling or wear. Cover is perfectly centered and flat. Staples are shiny and like new. the colors are intense and fresh.

Note: The condition of this comic is actually better than could normally be purchased from the newsstand.

Tiny color fleck

Flawless book - no defects.

GRADE: **MINT** (ONE - 99)

Example: Front cover of *The Amazing Spider-Man* #5, 1963. © Marvel Ent. Group.
Obvious defects: None.
Hidden defects: None.
OWL: 8.

Tight
spine

Tight
staple

Bindery corner   Flat with brilliant colors

Sharp corners

Tiny color fleck

Light
spine
stress

Bindery corner

A near perfect, flawless book.

Example: Front cover of Famous Funnies A Carnival Of Comics, 1933. © Famous Funnies.
Obvious defects: None.
Hidden defects: None.
OWL: 8.

Cover surface
is flawless

Spine is tight
and flat

Cover color is
bright and well
defined

Flat with
bright colors

Note: The survival of a pre-1935 comic book in this condition is nothing short of miraculous. The page quality of this example is OWL 8.

Mint (continued) - *Famous Funnies*
Example: Front cover close ups.

Extremely slight
corner abrasion

Sharp
corners

Tight
spine

GRADE: **MINT** (ONE - 98)

Example: Front cover of *Weird Comics* #1, 1939. © Fox Feat. Synd.
Obvious defects: None.
Hidden defects: Very slight foxing (see glossary) on margins of inside pages, typical of books from the "Larson" collection.
OWL: 7.

Intense, bright colors

No printing defects

Sharp corners

Clean, straight edges

Flat and clean

Note: This outstanding and rare example of an early 1940s comic book in Mint condition is from the famous "Lamont Larson" collection.

MINT (continued) - *Weird Comics*
Example: Front cover close ups.

Tiny corner tear

No binding
defects

Erased
name

Very slight corner tear

GRADE: **MINT** (ONE - 98)

Example: Front cover of *Red Ryder* #1, 1940, © Fred Harmon.
Obvious defects: Slight oxidation shadow (see glossary).
Hidden defects: Tiny corner piece missing from interior page.
OWL: 7.

Book-length oxidation
shadow along spine

Colors are
brilliant

All corners
are sharp

Spine is tight
and flat

Cover surface is
highly reflective

Note: This book is from a high grade #1 collection from Pennsylvania noted for covers
with very high reflectivity.

Book length oxidation shadow

Edges are clean
and straight

Tiny corner nick

Flat and excellent quality

GRADE: **MINT** (ONE - 98)

Example: Back cover of *Ace Comics* #95, 1945, © King Feat. Synd.
Obvious defects: None.
Hidden defects: None.
OWL: 7.

Bindery tear
(see glossary)

Bindery
tear

Note: Bindery corners commonly occur on vintage 68 page comic books of the 1930s and 1940s.

GRADE: **MINT** (ONE - 98)

Example: Front cover of *Dynamo* #2, 1966. © Tower Comics.
Obvious defects: None.
Hidden defects: None.
OWL: 8.

Note: This example is a "square bound" book (see glossary). Square bound comic books are notorious for having imperfect and/or incomplete spines because of the way they are constructed. The contraction of the glue used for binding the cover to the interior pages commonly wrinkles the spine. Additionally, simply opening a square bound comic book can degrade the spine and usually does. All these factors contribute to the rarity of high grade square bound comic books.

Staple
ridge

Spine is
complete,
unwrinkled
and flat.

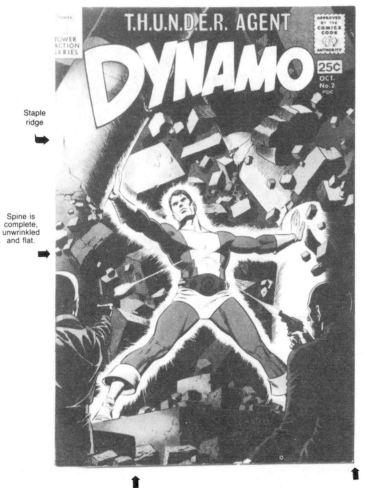

Exceptional color
brightness

All four corners
sharp and perfect

MINT (continued) - *Dynamo*
Example: Front cover close ups.

Tiny
corner tear

Staple
ridge

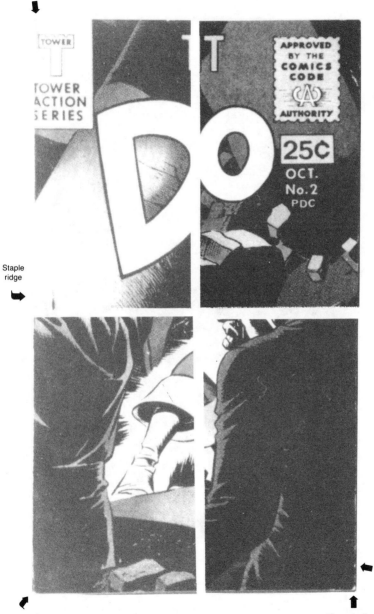

Slight bindery corner   Tiny color fleck

GRADE: **MINT** (ONE - 98)

Example: Front cover of *Captain America* #100, 1968. © Marvel Ent. Group.
Obvious defects: None.
Hidden defects: None.
OWL: 8.

Light
spine
crease

Tiny color fleck

Note: This book is still in its original newsstand condition as purchased from a comic book rack.

MINT (continued) - *Captain America*
Example: Front cover close ups.

Minor bindery trimming defect

Spine
stress
line

Tiny color fleck

67

GRADE: NEAR MINT
Abbreviated Notation: NM

Overstreet Numerical Equivalent (ONE) range: 97-90
(**Highest** possible NM grade = 97, **Mid**-grade = 94, **Lowest** possible NM grade = 90)

GRADE DESCRIPTION:
Beautiful, with only minor imperfections that keep it from the next higher grade. Minor imperfections that are allowed in this grade include tiny corner creases or staple stress lines, a few color flecks, bindery tears, tiny impact creases or a combination of the above where the overall eye appeal is less than Mint. Only the most subtle binding and/or printing defects allowed. Cover is flat with no surface wear. Cover inks are bright with high reflectivity and minimum of fading. Corners are cut square and sharp with ever so slight blunting permitted. Staples are generally centered, clean with only light rust, and no paper discoloration or staining. Cover is well centered and firmly secured to interior pages. Paper is supple and like new. Spine is tight and flat. In rare cases a comic was not stapled at the bindery and is not considered a defect. Any staple can be replaced on books up to FN, but only vintage staples to VF or NM. Mint books must have original staples.

CHECKLIST FOR THE GRADE NEAR MINT:

- ✓ Only minor imperfections noted.
- ✓ Almost no printing defects allowed.
- ✓ No bindery defects permitted in this grade except bindery tears (see glossary).
- ✓ Small and inconspicuously placed arrival dates and initials on cover are permitted.
- ✓ Cover is flat with no surface wear.
- ✓ Cover is bright.
- ✓ Cover is generally well centered.
- ✓ Staples are clean with no rust.
- ✓ Spine is flat and tight (no spine roll).
- ✓ Minute color fading is acceptable.
- ✓ No soiling, staining, or other discoloration.
- ✓ No hint of acidity in the odor of the newsprint.
- ✓ The overall look of a Near Mint condition comic book is "As if it were just purchased from the newsstand and read once or twice."

Note: Comic books published before 1970 in Near Mint condition are scarce. This grade is commonly viewed by the average collector as the best grade obtainable.

⚠ **COLLECTOR ALERT:** Collectors should thoroughly examine any book touted to be in this grade. Further, they should be carefully scrutinized for restoration.

⚠ **COLLECTOR ALERT:** Expensive/key comic books listed as being in "high grade" often have some restoration. In most cases restoration performed on otherwise near mint books will reduce the grade. A Very Fine comic book **cannot** be transformed into a near mint comic book through restoration.

GRADE: **NEAR MINT** (ONE - 97)

Example: Front cover of *Special Edition Comics* #1, 1940. © Fawcett Publ.
Obvious defects: None.
Hidden defects: None.
OWL: 7.

Very light corner abrasion

Sharp corners

Tight staple

Tight staple

Light book-length dust shadow

Note: This rare example is one of the best known copies and is from a high grade Pennsylvania collection where all the issues had an "x" with the arrival date.

Very
light
dust
shadow

Pencilled arrival date

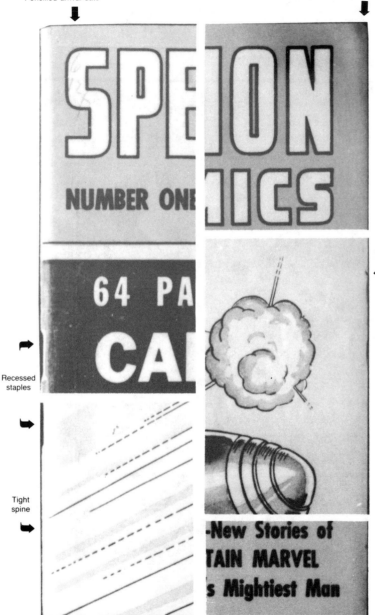

Tiny
edge
dent

Recessed
staples

Tight
spine

-New Stories of
TAIN MARVEL
s Mightiest Man

GRADE: **NEAR MINT** (ONE - **97**)

Example: Front cover of *Superman* #53, 1948. © DC Comics.
Obvious defects: None.
Hidden defects: None.
OWL: 8.

Sharp corner

Light
rusty
staple

Light
rusty
staple

Bindery defect, type 1b

Tiny, very light corner crease

NEAR MINT (continued) - *Superman*
Example: Front cover close ups.

Sharp corner

Light
rusty
staple

Very light tiny corner crease

GRADE: **NEAR MINT** (ONE - 96)

Example: Front cover of *Blue Ribbon* #1, 1939. © MLJ.

Obvious defects: None.

Hidden defects: Bindery defect - Pressure from lateral bar (see glossary) of lower staple has partially separated cover at spine.

OWL: 8.

Sharp corners

Very light edge warping

Tight staple

Tight spine

Tight staple

Very light crease

Sharp corners

Note: This outstanding example is from the famous "Denver" collection. Pre-1940 comic books in this condition are extremely rare.

NEAR MINT (continued) - *Blue Ribbon Comics*
Example: Front cover close ups.

Bindery
corner

Very slight
edge warping

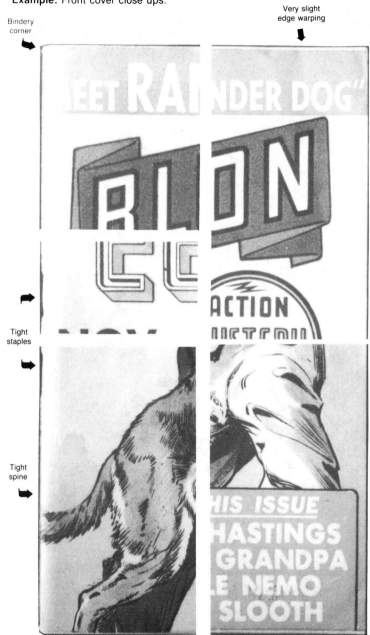

Tight
staples

Tight
spine

GRADE: **NEAR MINT** (ONE - 96)

Example: Front cover of *All Good Comics* nn, 1944. © Fox Feat. Synd.
Obvious defects: None.
Hidden defects: Transfer stain on inside front cover (see glossary).
OWL: 7.

Tiny
corner nick

Minor edge wrinkling

Staple
ridge

Staple
ridge

Perfect square bound spine

Note: Rare example of a pre-1945 square bound comic book with a perfect, unwrinkled and complete spine. Variable whiteness level on inside pages ranging from OWL 6 to Owl 8.

Tiny corner nick

Minor edge wrinkling

Sharp corner

Normal wavy surface along spine

Staple ridge

Staple ridge

Sharp
corner

Tiny
piece out

Staple
ridge

Heavy
object
crease

Staple
ridge

GRADE: **NEAR MINT** (ONE - **96**)

Example: Front cover of *Straight Arrow* #7, 1950. © Magazine Enterpises.

Obvious defects: None.

Hidden defects: None.

OWL: 8.

Small color scrape

Transparent cover (see glossary)

Tiny staple stress

Light spine stress lines

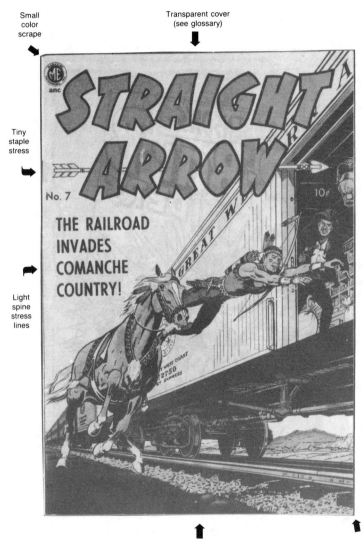

Flat and excellent

Sharp corners

Note: Western comic books in this grade are very rare.

GRADE: **NEAR MINT** (ONE - 96)

Example: Front cover of *Strange Worlds* #5, 1951. © Avon.
Obvious defects: None.
Hidden defects: None.
OWL: 8.

Tiny color
fleck

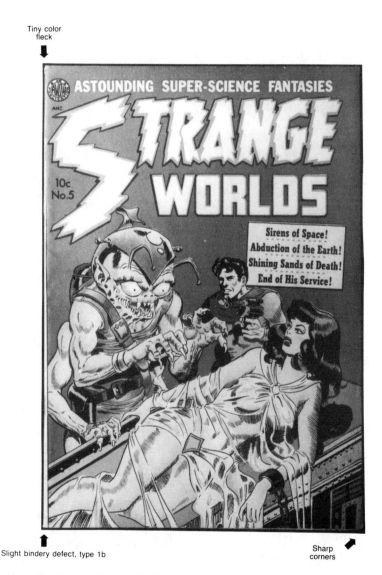

Slight bindery defect, type 1b

Sharp
corners

Note: Comic books from the 1950s rarely occur in high grade. This exceptional copy is from the "White Mountain" collection (see glossary), Overstreet Whiteness Level (OWL) of 9.

Tiny
color fleck

Total absence of abrasion
on spine and cover

Very tiny
corner crease

Tight
staple

All edges are sharp
and well defined

GRADE: **NEAR MINT** (ONE - 96)

Example: Front cover of *Fox And The Crow* #1, 1952. © DC Comics.
Obvious defects: None.
Hidden defects: None.
OWL: 7.

Progressive bindery defect 1b (see glossary). Part of back cover shows along spine of front cover.

All four corners are sharp and well defined

Note: This comic book would rank higher if not for bindery defect.

Bindery defect

Tiny
spine
tear

Very light edge crease

Slight maverick signature visible

GRADE: **NEAR MINT** (ONE - **96**)

Example: Front cover of *Adventures Into Weird Worlds* #6, 1952. © Marvel Comics.
Obvious defects: None.
Hidden defects: Centerfold loose from lower staple.
OWL: 9.

Excellent quality and perfect except for bindery defect

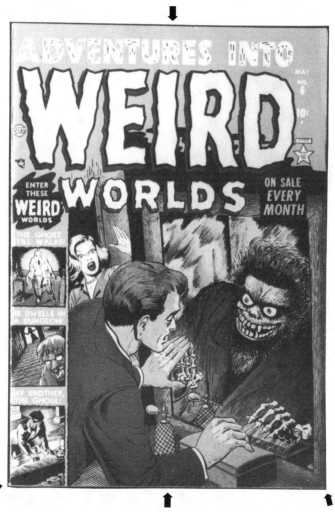

Tiny
color
fleck

See notation under "Black Cover"
in glossary

Corners are
sharp and
well defined

Note: As with most Precode 1950s comic books, Atlas horror comics (see glossary) are notoriously difficult to find in high grade with good paper quality. This exceptional example is from the "White Mountain" collection (see glossary).

Tiny color fleck

Tiny color fleck

Tiny color fleck

Tiny color fleck

GRADE: **NEAR MINT** (ONE - 96)

Example: Front cover of *The Amazing Spider-Man* Annual #2, 1965. © Marvel Comics.
Obvious defects: None.
Hidden defects: Siamese pages (see glossary).
OWL: 8.

All corners
are sharp

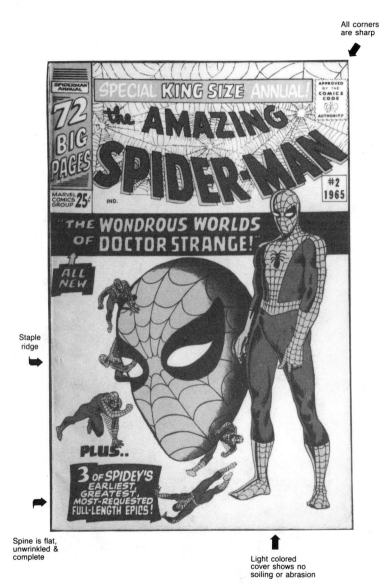

Staple
ridge

Spine is flat,
unwrinkled &
complete

Light colored
cover shows no
soiling or abrasion

Note: This example is a square bound comic book from the mid-1960s with the usual potential for spine problems. This superb copy sports a near perfect spine (see spine nick on next page).

NEAR MINT (continued) - *The Amazing Spider-Man*
Example: Front cover close ups.

Tiny corner
nick

Normal
waviness
due to
improper
glue
application

Light corner crease

GRADE: **NEAR MINT** (ONE - 95)

Example: Front cover of *Fantastic Comics* #1, 1939. © Fox Publ.
Obvious defects: None.
Hidden defects: None.
OWL: 8.

Bindery
corner

Sharp corner

Tight
staples

Tight
spine

Bindery
corner

Flat and excellent

Sharp
corner

Note: This rare comic book is from the famous "Lamont Larson" collection.

Erased number
(top of letter A)

Sharp corner

Recessed
staples

Bindery corner

Tiny corner crease

GRADE: **NEAR MINT** (ONE - 94)

Example: Front cover of *Sure-Fire Comics* #3, 1940. © ACE
Obvious defects: None.
Hidden defects: None.
OWL: 8.

Light
foxing
along
spine
➡

Tight
staple
➡

Name
pencilled
on cover
➡

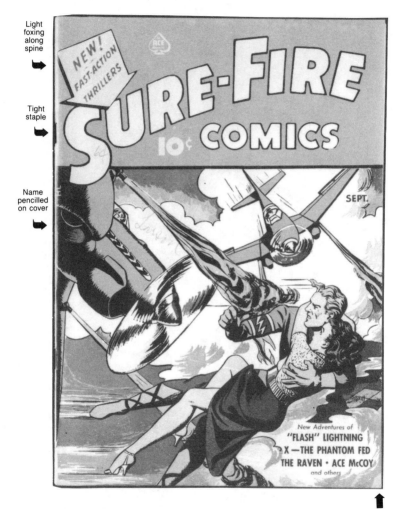

Sharp
corners

Note: This example is from the famous "Lamont Larson" collection. Comic books from this collection typically have varying amounts of foxing (see glossary) on covers and interior pages.

NEAR MINT (continued) - *Sure Fire Comics*
Example: Front cover close ups.

All sharp corners

Light foxing along top edge

Light foxing along spine

Tight staple

New Adventures of
"LASH" LIGHTNING
-THE PHANTOM FED
RAVEN • ACE McCOY
and others

NEAR MINT (continued) - *Sure Fire Comics*
Example: Back cover.

Note: The foxing is the primary defect which lowered the grade from the high end of the NM range to the middle of the NM range.

GRADE: **NEAR MINT** (ONE - 94)

Example: Front cover of Marvel Mystery #16. 1941. © Marvel Comics.
Obvious defects: None.
Hidden defects: None.
OWL: 8.

Cover color is bright and well defined

Heavy object crease

Tiny color fleck

No printing defects

Spine is tight and flat

No binding defects

Tiny color fleck

Corners are sharp

This book has brilliant colors, perfect flatness, tight staples and spine and fresh off-white pages.

NEAR MINT (continued) - *Marvel Mystery Comics*
Example: Front cover close ups.

Heavy object crease

Bindery
corner

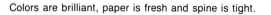

Bindery
corner

Perfect corners

Colors are brilliant, paper is fresh and spine is tight.

GRADE: **NEAR MINT** (ONE - 92)

Example: Front cover of *Ghost Rider* #16, 1991. © Marvel Ent. Group.
Obvious defects: None.
Hidden defects: None.
OWL: 10.

Double cover

UPC code

Note: This is an example of a comic book with a double cover. Multiple covers occur frequently and enhance the desirability of comics.

GRADE: **NEAR MINT** (ONE - **91**)

Example: Front cover of *Strange Tales* #81, 1961. © Marvel Comics.
Obvious defects: None.
Hidden defects: Two maverick pages (see glossary).
OWL: 9.

Creases caused by impact at edge

Color flecks

Tiny transverse spine crease

Note: This example is from the "White Mountain" collection, noted for exceptional paper quality.

Creases caused by impact at edge

Sharp, well defined corner

Color flecks

Tiny transverse spine crease

GRADE: VERY FINE
Abbreviated Notation: VF

Overstreet Numerical Equivalent (ONE) range: 89-75
(**Highest** possible VF grade = 89, **Mid**-grade = 82, **Lowest** possible VF grade = 75)

GRADE DESCRIPTION:
An excellent copy with above average eye appeal. Sharp, bright and clean with supple pages. Cover is relatively flat with minimal surface wear beginning to show. Cover inks are generally bright with moderate to high reflectivity. Slight wear beginning to show including some minute wear at corners. Staples may show some discoloration. Spine may have a few transverse stress lines but is relatively flat. A light ½ inch crease is acceptible. A comic book in this grade has the appearance of having been carefully handled. Pages and covers can be yellowish/tannish (at the least) but not brown.

CHECKLIST FOR THE GRADE VERY FINE:

- ✓ Outstanding eye appeal.
- ✓ Minor printing defects are allowed.
- ✓ Minor bindery defects are allowed.
- ✓ Cover is relatively flat with minimal surface wear.
- ✓ Cover inks are generally bright.
- ✓ Some slight wear on cover, at spine and at corners beginning to show.
- ✓ Staples may show some discoloration.
- ✓ Spine is relatively flat with a few transverse stress lines.
- ✓ No obvious visible soiling, staining, or other discoloration, except for minor staple rust migration.
- ✓ Minor corner creasing is allowed.
- ✓ Interior pages can be yellowish/tannish, but not brown.

Note: Comic books in this grade are normally the highest grade offered for sale.

⚠ *COLLECTOR ALERT*: Collectors should thoroughly examine any book touted to be in this grade. Further, they should be carefully scrutinized for restoration.

⚠ *COLLECTOR ALERT:* Many books graded higher than VF are, in reality, misgraded and are actually in VF condition.

GRADE: **VERY FINE** (ONE - 88)

Example: Front cover of *Comic Cavalcade* #11, 1945. © DC Comics.
Obvious defects: None.
Hidden defects: Minor discoloration at bottom of inside back cover.
OWL: 8.

Sharp corner

All corners
are sharp

Staple
ridge

Pencilled
initial

Staple
ridge

Spine is slightly wrinkled but complete

Sharp corner

Note: This example is a 1940s square bound. Typically the spine on these comic books is incomplete. The most common location of spine defects is at the corners. Additionally, square bound comics usually have a "reading crease" (see glossary) due to over-gluing of the spine. **Caution:** The collector should be careful not to open the cover of a square bound comic more than about 45 degrees in order to prevent reading creases and possible spine damage.

VERY FINE (continued) - *Comic Cavalcade*
Example: Front cover close ups.

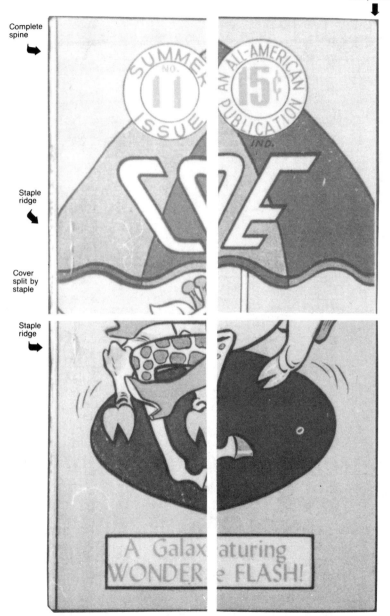

GRADE: **VERY FINE** (ONE - 86)

Example: Front cover of *The Comics Magazine* #2, 1936. © Comics Magazine.
Obvious defects: None.
Hidden defects: Nearly invisible stains on cover.
OWL: 8.

Note: This extremely rare comic book was published with a newsprint cover. Therefore the reflectivity was low due to the absorptive nature of the paper. Newsprint cover comics of the 1930s are virtually non-existant in high grade. Those known to exist are usually restored.

Note: The cover and the two interior 32 page signatures were each trimmed independently of each other before the assembly process. Because of this the pages are uneven at the bottom. Slightly protruding interior pages have a higher incidence of impact damage, oxidation and discoloration.

Bindery corner

Sharp corner

Clean, off-centered staples

Clean staples

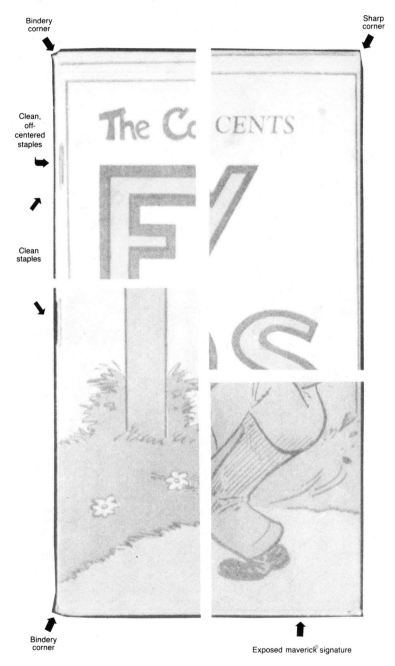

Bindery corner

Exposed maverick signature

GRADE: **VERY FINE** (ONE - 86)

Example: Front cover of *Detective Comics* #24, 1939. © DC Comics.
Obvious defects: None.
Hidden defects: Small repair inside top of spine.
OWL: 6.

Tiny tear with webbing repair on inside

Very light corner flecks

Sharp corner

Recessed staple

Recessed staple

Tiny edge tear

Sharp corner

VERY FINE (continued) - *Detective Comics*
Example: Front cover close ups.

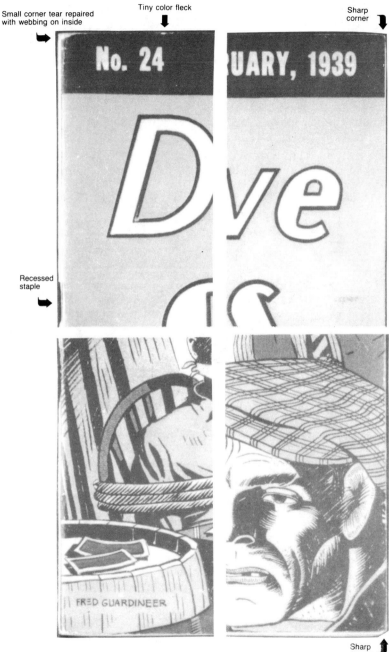

Small corner tear repaired with webbing on inside

Tiny color fleck

Sharp corner

Recessed staple

Sharp corner

Bindery corner with webbing repair

Sharp corner

Very light dust shadow

Sharp corner

Faint dust shadow

GRADE: **VERY FINE** (ONE - **86**)

Example: Front cover of *Superman* #57, 1949. © DC Comics.
Obvious defects: None.
Hidden defects: Slight tanning at the bottom of interior pages. Tiny corner missing,
one interior page.
OWL: 6.

Brilliant colors, flat and clean

No top staple

Tiny tear

Bindery tear

Sharp corners

Sharp corner

Very light soiling along edges

Edge
wrinkle

Small
light
corner
fold

Tiny
tear

GRADE: **VERY FINE** (ONE - 86)

Example: Front cover of *Green Lantern* #1, 1960. © DC Comics.
Obvious defects: None.
Hidden defects: None.
OWL: 7.

Sharp
corners

Spine
stress

Tight
spine

Very slight corner abrasion

VERY FINE (continued) - *Green Lantern*
Example: Front cover close ups.

Over-cover (see glossary)-Top of cover extends
1/16th inch past the edge of interior pages

Edge dent

Spine
stress

Spine
stress

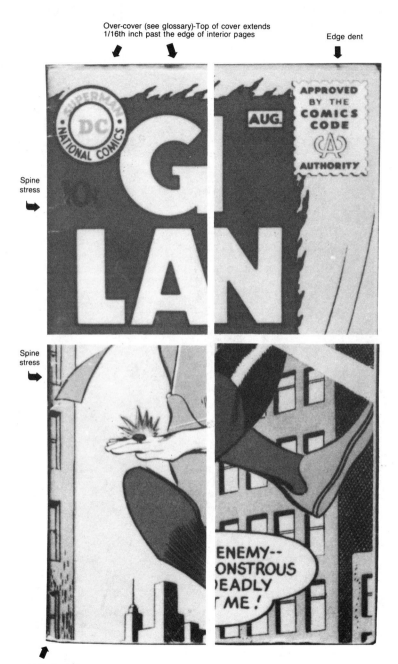

Light abraded corner

GRADE: **VERY FINE** (ONE - **82**)

Example: Front cover of *Detective Comics* #31, 1939. © DC Comics.
Obvious defects: None.
Hidden defects: None.
OWL: 7.

Sharp corner

Erased grease initial

Light edge stress

Sharp corner

Flat and clean

Sharp corner

Very light
edge stress

Tight
staple

Tight
spine

Tiny
tear

Light
book-
length
dust
shadow

Sharp corner

GRADE: **VERY FINE** (ONE - **78**)

Example: Front cover of *John Wayne Adventure Comics* #9, 1951. © Toby Press.
Obvious defects: Sun Shadow.
Hidden defects: Light tanning around in cover edges.
OWL: 6.

Oxidation
shadow

Sharp corners

Spine
creases

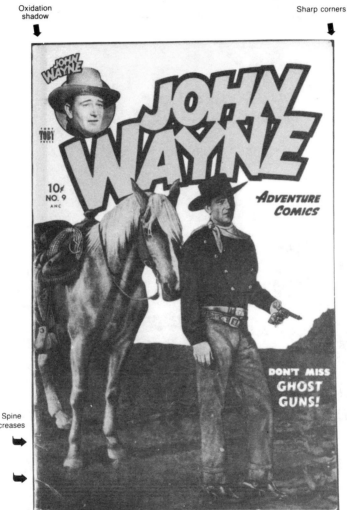

Note: This book has brilliant colors, is flat with clean pages. The oxidation shadow defect drops the grade by 5-7 points.

GRADE: **VERY FINE** (ONE - **77**)

Example: Front cover of *Nellie The Nurse* #7, 1947. © Marvel Ent.
Obvious defects: None.
Hidden defects: Maverick page (see glossary).
OWL: 7.

Bindery tear   Light book-length crease

Pencilled
initial

Color
scrape

Light
abraded
corner

All corners
are sharp

VERY FINE (continued) - *Nellie The Nurse*
Example: Front cover close ups.

Bindery tear

Light sun shadow

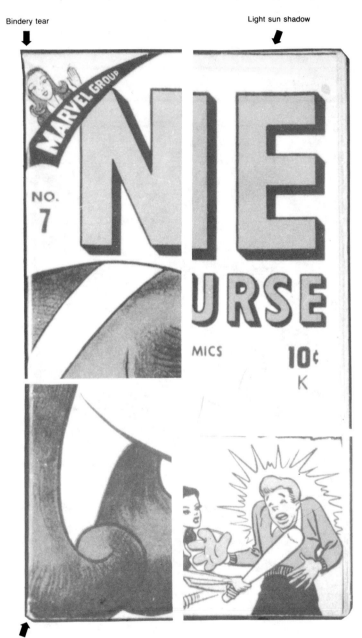

Minor corner abrasion

Very light soiling
on cover

Very
light
soiling
around
staple

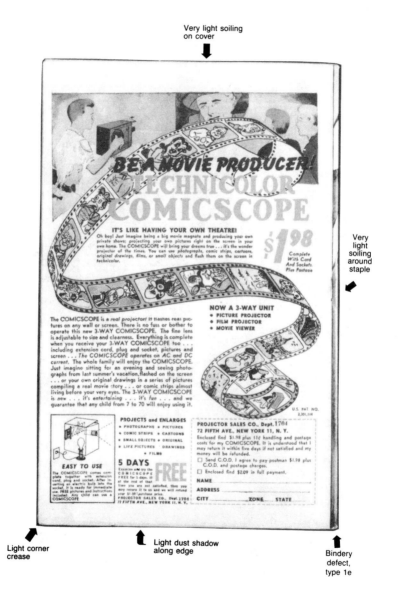

Light corner
crease

Light dust shadow
along edge

Bindery
defect,
type 1e

GRADE: **VERY FINE** (ONE - 75)

Example: Front cover of *Batman* #153, 1963. © DC Comics.
Obvious defects: None.
Hidden defects: Transfer stain (see glossary), inside front and back covers. Stains on outside back cover penetrate to inside back cover.
OWL: 6.

Tiny color fleck

All four corners are fairly sharp

Spine stress

Minor blunted corner

Light crease line

VERY FINE (continued) - *Batman*
Example: Front cover close ups.

Minor
blunted
corner

Staple
stress
line

Small
staple
tear

Spine
crease

Light stress line

Clean edges

Note: This book would have graded ONE-82 if not for the staining on the back cover.

GRADE: **VERY FINE** (ONE - 75)

Example: Front cover to *Mystery In Space* #91, 1964. © DC Comics.
Obvious defects: None.
Hidden defects: Sharp object penetrated cover and first 12 pages.
OWL: 8.

Very light
edge wear

Multiple
transverse
spine
creases

Abraded corner

Light foxing along edge

VERY FINE (continued) - *Mystery In Space*
Example: Front cover close ups.

Light abraded corner

Spine stress

Edge stress lines

Stress line

Spine stress lines

Light abraded corner

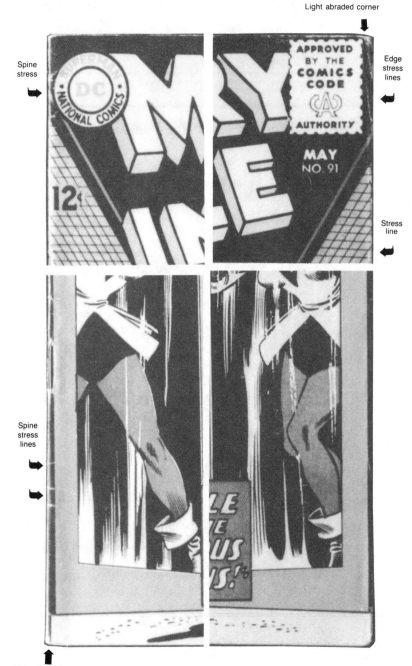

GRADE: VERY FINE
DEFECT SECTION

The grade of all of the books in this section has (a) dropped from either a higher grade to the Very Fine grade due to a specific damaging defect, or (b) has dropped a few points within the same grade.

Publishers
cover
stamp

Defect: Publishers cover stamp. When not obtrusive this defect does not change the grade. Some collectors feel that it enhances the value.

Defect: Maverick staple which did not completely penetrate the cover. Grade before defect - NM96. Grade with defect - VF89. *Ghost Rider #4*, 1991. © Marvel Ent. Group.

Maverick
staple

Bindery defect,
type 1a

Defect: Bindery defect type 1a. Grade before defect - NM95. Grade with defect - VF87. *Roly Poly Comics #10*, 1946. © Green Publishing Co.

Detached cover at staple

Defect: Cover detached at lower staple. Grade before defect - NM95. Grade with defect VF85. Very common defect in all 32 page books from this period due to thin cover stock. *Justice League Of America #9*, 1962. © DC Comics.

Price sticker

Defect: Price sticker on cover. Grade before defect - NM94. Grade with defect - VF84. (note: This example is from the Nashville, TN "Bus Stop" collection) *Batman #152*, 1962. © DC Comics.

Defect: Abraded spine corner. Grade before defect - NM94. Grade with defect - VF82. *Mystic Comics* #9, 1942. © Marvel Ent. Group.

Abraded corner

Mailing seal on edge

Defect: Paper mailing seal on right edge. This is a premium comic that was mailed unprotected. Since all copies have this defect, it does not change the grade. Grade is VF82. *Tom Mix* #3, © Ralston.

Defect: Inside cover of a double cover comic with a bindery defect maverick cover at bottom of spine. Grade before defect - NM94. Grade with defect - VF80. *Ghost Rider* #16, 1991. © Marvel Ent. Group.

Small corner crease

Defect: Small corner crease. Grade before defect - NM93. Grade with defect - VF78. *Star Trek* #21, 1973. © Paramount Pic. Corp.

Cover trimmed here

Defect: Bindery trim defect type 1d (see glossary). Grade before defect - VF88. Grade with defect - VF77. *Ace comics* #121, 1947. © King Feat.

File copy stamp

Defect: Lloyd Jacques File Copy stamp. Grade before defect - VF82. Grade with defect - VF77. *Smash Comics #63*, 1946. © Quality Comics.

Oxidation shadow

Defect: Oxidation shadow along right edge. Grade before defect - NM94. Grade with defect VF77. *Single Series #2*, 1939. © United Feat. Synd.

Close up of edge tears

Defect: Cover edge trimming tears caused by a dull paper cutter at the bindery. Grade without defect - VF85. Grade with defect - VF75. *All-American Comics #28*, 1941. © DC Comics.

Edge tears

Initial and date stamp

Defect: Date stamp and initial on cover. Grade before defect - VF82. Grade with defect - VF76. *Star Spangled Comics #10*, 1943. © DC Comics.

Trim defect

Defect: Bindery trimming defect type 2a (see glossary). Grade without defect - VF82. Grade with defect - VF76. *Ace Comics #75*, 1943. © King Feat. Synd.

GRADE: FINE
Abbreviated Notation: FN

Overstreet Numerical Equivalent (ONE) range: 74-55
(**Highest** possible FN grade = 74, **Mid**-grade = 65, **Lowest** possible FN grade = 55)

GRADE DESCRIPTION:
An exceptional, above average copy that shows minor wear but is still relatively flat and clean with no major creasing or other serious defects. Eye appeal is somewhat reduced because of surface wear and the accumulation of small defects, especially on the spine and edges. Centerfold may be loose but not detached. A Fine condition comic book shows handling. Compared to a VF, cover inks are beginning to show a reduction in reflectivity but is still highly collectible and desirable.

CHECKLIST FOR THE GRADE FINE:

- Average eye appeal.
- Minor wear visible.
- Minor creasing is allowed.
- Accumulation of small defects on spine and edge(s).
- Blunted corners more common.
- Minor staining and discoloration that does not significantly reduce eye appeal.
- Staples may show moderate discoloration.
- Interior pages may have small tears in the margins or blunted corners.
- Staple tears are common.
- Spines may have transverse stress creases.
- Interior pages can be tan/brown.
- A minor spine roll is allowed.

Note: Fine has historically been the most difficult grade to identify. It is the highest grade which allows a *wide range* of defects to occur.

⚒ **COLLECTOR ALERT:** Many books offered for sale are inaccurately graded as Fine. Collectors should carefully examine all books labeled with this grade for brittle or extremely brown pages.

GRADE: **FINE** (ONE - 71)

Example: Front cover of *Spy Cases* #26, 1950. © Marvel Ent. Group.
Obvious defects: None.
Hidden defects: Transfer stain (see glossary), inside back cover. Moderate staple discoloration at centerfold.
OWL: 6.

FINE (continued) - *Spy Cases*
Example: Front cover close ups.

FINE (continued) - *Spy Cases*
Example: Back cover.

Tiny corner crease

Edge
tear

Minor cover soiling

Minor
stress
marks &
soiling

Minor soiling and corner fold

GRADE: **FINE** (ONE - 68)

Example: Front cover of *Adventure Comics* #79, 1942. © DC Comics.
Obvious defects: None.
Hidden defects: None.
OWL: 6.

Small corner tear

Small edge tear

Light dust shadow

Bindery corner

Light rounded corner

FINE (continued) - *Adventure Comics*
Example: Front cover close ups.

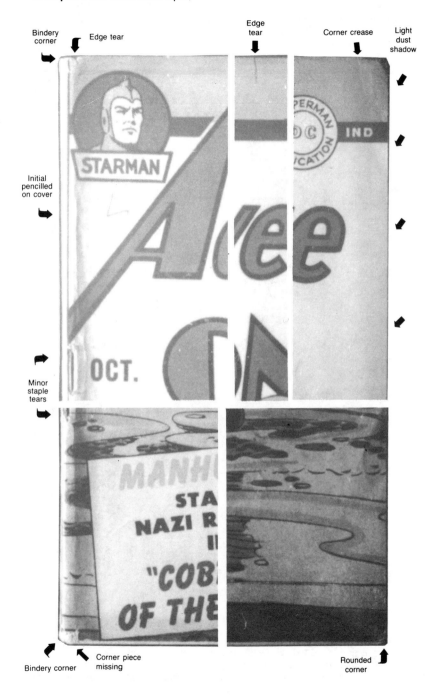

Bindery corner

Edge tear

Edge tear

Corner crease

Light dust shadow

Initial pencilled on cover

Minor staple tears

Bindery corner

Corner piece missing

Rounded corner

GRADE: **FINE** (ONE - 65)

Example: Front cover to *New Book Of Comics* #2, 1938. © DC Comics.
Obvious defects: None.
Hidden defects: Cover is partially separated from the interior pages at the spine.
OWL: 7.

Abraded corner

Color fleck

Light corner crease

Abraded corner

Note: This rare comic book is (a) the third DC annual, (b) the second standard sized DC annual, (c) the second square bound comic book ever published. The covers are made from thick poster board which is glued to the interior pages. The cover has a tendency to separate from interior pages when it is opened more than 30 degrees.

FINE (continued) - *New Book Of Comics*
Example: Front cover close ups.

Abraded spine

Color flecks

Very light corner crease

Color fleck

Transverse spine creases

Abraded corner

Light corner creases

GRADE: **FINE** (ONE - 65)

Example: Front cover of *Showcase* #13, 1958. © DC Comics.
Obvious defects: None.
Hidden defects: None.
OWL: 7.

Edge tear

Sharp corner

Abraded
staple
holes

Bindery defect, type 1b

Light corner crease

FINE (continued) - *Showcase*
Example: Front cover close ups.

Abraded corner

Edge tear

Abraded
staple
holes

Staple
tears

Spine
stress
lines

Impacted corner

GRADE: **FINE** (ONE - 60)

Example: Front cover of *Ace Comics* #5, 1937. © King Feat. Synd.
Obvious defects: None.
Hidden defects: None.
OWL: 6.

Bindery corner

Very minor color flecks along edge

Book-length cover wrinkle caused by dampness (not a crease).

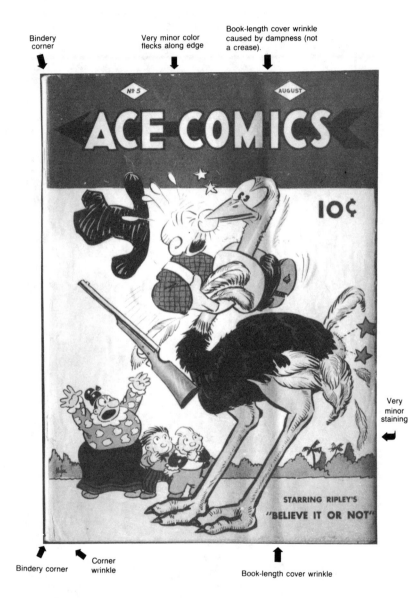

Very minor staining

Bindery corner

Corner wrinkle

Book-length cover wrinkle

FINE (continued) - *Ace Comics*
Example: Front cover close ups.

Very minor abraded corner

Edge stress line

Very minor color flecks

Tiny color fleck

Small staple tears

Small corner piece out

Book-length wrinkle

Exposed maverick signature

FINE (continued) - *Ace Comics*
Example: Back cover.

Nice, white, flat cover

Light
corner
crease

Very white, clean back cover

Bindery
corner

GRADE: **FINE** (ONE - 60)

Example: Front cover of *Detective Comics* #22, 1938. © DC Comics.
Obvious defects: None.
Hidden defects: Centerfold detached at lower staple.
OWL: 5.

Minor sealed
edge tear

Tiny color fleck

Tiny
color
fleck

Edge
tear

Tiny
spine
scrape

Staple
tear

FINE (continued) - *Detective Comics*
Example: Front cover close ups.

¼'' spine tear
repaired with tape

Tiny
color
fleck

Minor
color
fleck

Tear

Minor
soiling

Minor
edge
wear

Abraded
corner

Minor edge wear

GRADE: FINE (ONE - 60)

Example: Front cover of *Real Screen Comics* #34, 1951. © DC Comics.
Obvious defects: None.
Hidden defects: Off-center upper staple.
OWL: 6.

Progressive
bindery
trimming
defect

Store
stamp

Very light
corner crease

FINE (continued) - *Real Screen Comics*
Example: Front cover close ups.

Progressive bindery trimming
defect, type 1b (see glossary)

Store
stamp

Tiny
tear

Tiny corner chip

Light corner crease

GRADE: **FINE** (ONE - 60)

Example: Front cover of *Rip Hunter... Time Master* #1, 1961. © DC Comics
Obvious defects: None.
Hidden defects: None.
OWL: 8.

Inked
date
stamp

Edge
stress

Edge tear

FINE (continued) - *Rip Hunter... Time Master*
Example: Front cover close ups.

Bindery defect, type 1a

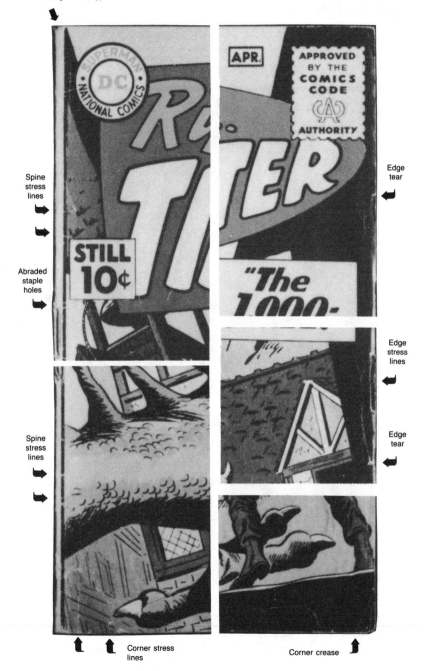

Spine stress lines

Abraded staple holes

Spine stress lines

Edge tear

Edge stress lines

Edge tear

Corner stress lines

Corner crease

GRADE: FINE (ONE - 58)

Example: Front cover of *Archie's Christmas Stocking* #1, 1954. © Archie Publ.
Obvious defects: None.
Hidden defects: None.
OWL: 6.

Minor stress lines

Small, light corner crease

Long stratified multiple reading creases

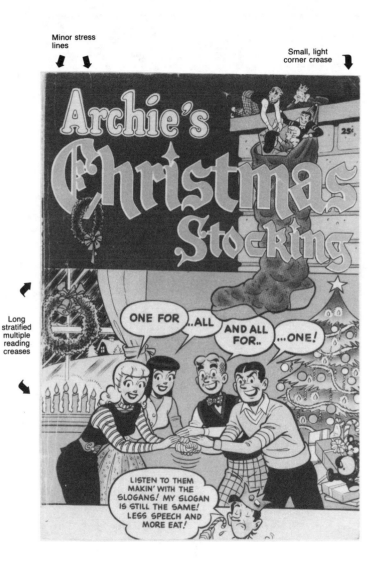

FINE (continued) - *Archie's Christmas Stocking*
Example: Front cover close ups.

Light abraded corner

Stress creases

Tiny tear

Minor corner crease

Multiple reading creases

Corner tear and abrasion

GRADE: **FINE** (ONE - 56)

Example: Front cover of *Showcase* #10, 1957. © DC Comics.
Obvious defects: None.
Hidden defects: None.
OWL: 6.

Sharp corner

Edge stress line

Tiny corner crease

Edge stress line

Spine stress line

Light staple tears

Small corner tear

Light corner crease

GRADE: **FINE** (ONE - 56)

Example: Front cover of *Brave And The Bold* #28, 1960. © DC Comics.
Obvious defects: None.
Hidden defects: None.
OWL: 8.

Cover has very
minor stress lines

Light
wear
around
staple

Small
staple
tear

Small tear

FINE (continued) - *Brave And The Bold*
Example: Front cover close ups.

Light abraded corner

Minor stress lines

Spine stress lines

APPROVED BY THE COMICS CODE AUTHORITY

THE WORLD'S GREATEST HEROES TEAM UP TO BATTLE

STARRO QUEROR!

Slight abraded spine

Minor wear & stress

Abraded corner

Stress line

Very light crease line

Slightly rounded corner

GRADE: **FINE** (ONE - 55)

Example: Front cover of *World's Finest Comics* #10, 1943. © DC Comics.
Obvious defects: None.
Hidden defects: Browning inside covers at bottom (Owl-3).
OWL: 7.

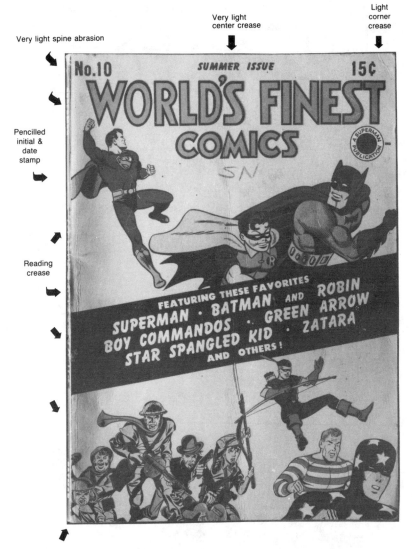

Light corner crease

Very light center crease

Very light spine abrasion

Pencilled initial & date stamp

Reading crease

Light spine abrasion

Note: This is an example of an early 1940s square bound comic book. Covers are made from thick poster board which is very easily creased when the book is read.

FINE (continued) - *World's Finest Comics*
Example: Front cover close ups.

Very light corner crease

Color chip

Minor wrinkle

No.10   15¢

Book-length reading crease

Light Corner crease

Light spine abrasion   Multiple creases

Minor stress mark

Minor edge wear

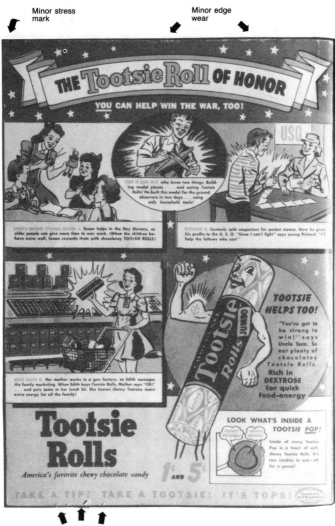

Color flecks

GRADE: FINE
DEFECT SECTION

The grade of all of the books in this section have (a) dropped from either a higher grade to the Fine grade due to a specific damaging defect, or (b) have dropped a few points within this grade.

Pencilled arrival date

Medium dust shadow

Defect: Dust shadow and pencilled arrival date on cover does not affect this grade. *Superman* #3, 1940. © DC Comics.

Pencilled initials & light date stamp

Defect: Two sets of pencilled initials and light date stamp. No affect on this grade. *Sub-Mariner Comics #12*, 1943-44. © Marvel Ent. Group.

Neatly placed name stamp

Defect: Neat name stamp. No affect on this grade. *Sharp Comics #2*, 1946. © H.C. Blakerby.

Close up to show blurred out of register printing.

Defect: Out of register printing. Grade without defect - VF82. Grade with defect - FN74. *Atomic Comics* #4, 1946. © Green Publ.

Store
stamp

Defect: Neatly placed date stamp. No affect on this grade. *Target Comics* V10#2, 1949. © Novelty Press.

Date
stamp

Defect: Neat date stamp. Unobtrusive placement of stamp does not affect this grade. *Batman #73*, 1952. © DC Comics.

NEW *OVERSTREET* COMIC BOOK GRADING CARD!!
You get two cards in one—The ONE/OWL CARD!

COMIC BOOK GRADING CARD

THE ONE CARD
OVERSTREET'S NUMERICAL EQUIVALENT

NUMERICAL GRADE

Grade (abbrev.)	High	Center	Low	Point spread
Mint (MT)	100	99	98	(3)
Near Mint (NM)	97	94	90	(8)
Very Fine (VF)	89	82	75	(15)
Fine (FN)	74	65	55	(20)
Very Good (VG)	54	45	35	(20)
Good (GD)	34	25	15	(20)
Fair (FR)	14	10	5	(10)
Poor (PR)	4	3	1	(4)

Most common occurrence

This card shows each comic book grade and its numerical equivalent (ONE) range. Consult Overstreet's Comic Book Grading Guide for grading criteria and instructions on the use of this card. Additional cards may be purchased.

Overstreet Publications, Inc.
780 Hunt Cliff Dr. NW. Cleveland, TN 37311.

Robert M. Overstreet, all rights reserved.

INCHES   1   2

ABOUT THE ONE CARD
(front side-facsimile, not for use)

With the recent development of the **Overstreet 100 point grading system**, it became clear that a reference tool **(THE ONE CARD)** was needed so that collectors could quickly and easily convert the traditional grading terms (*Mint, Near Mint, Very Fine, Fine, Very Good, Good, Fair & Poor*) to the numerical grading system. **THE ONE CARD** was created for this purpose and a likeness is provided here for your use as you become more familiar with the art of grading comic books. Note that the grades Good, Very Good and Fine have been emphasized because they repreent the condition in which comic books are most often found. Comic books in these grades also have the potential for the most defect combinations. Their expanded point ranges reflect this.

The higher grades, however, have been assigned a graduating smaller point range as the allowable defects drop and less points are needed in those grades. Conversely, the lower grades need a graduating smaller point range since more and more defects are allowed which do not change these grades.

HOW TO USE THIS CARD: This card is used in conjunction with the **Overstreet Comic Book Grading Guide.** The numerical system is easily referenced with the hundreds of detailed photos of comic book covers in all grades.

ABOUT THE OWL CARD
(back side—facsimile, not for use)

Modern comic book grading now requires the description of the color of comic book paper and "whiteness level." For the first time, comic book collectors will be able to accurately describe the paper color/quality in a standardized way by utilizing **THE OWL CARD.**

For your convenience, each color range has been assigned a value with the most desirable state of paper preservation being assigned a value of 10 (new comic books). Each color has a single number or a range of numbers. The numbers along both edges of **THE OWL CARD** represent the lowest acceptable number for that color.

It is important to note that the average "whiteness level" of comic books is **OWL5.**

Brittle (a condition of paper, not a color) has been given a value of 0. All comic books with brittle paper would be graded **OWL0.**

HOW TO USE THE OWL CARD: Simply place the color bands over the edge of the inside paper of your comic book and match up the color. Usually the actual color will fall between the **OWL** numbers and will have to be interpolated. This number should be used with the **ONE** number to completely describe a comic book's condition.

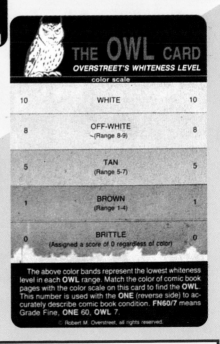

THE OWL CARD
OVERSTREET'S WHITENESS LEVEL
color scale

10	WHITE	10
8	OFF-WHITE (Range 8-9)	8
5	TAN (Range 5-7)	5
1	BROWN (Range 1-4)	1
0	BRITTLE (Assigned a score of 0 regardless of color)	0

The above color bands represent the lowest whiteness level in each **OWL** range. Match the color of comic book pages with the color scale on this card to find the **OWL.** This number is used with the **ONE** (reverse side) to accurately describe comic book condition. **FN60/7** means Grade Fine, **ONE 60, OWL 7.**

© Robert M. Overstreet, all rights reserved.

HOW TO GET YOUR OWN PERSONAL *OVERSTREET* GRADING CARD

Yes, send me . . . . **GRADING CARDS.** I have enclosed . . . . Price: $2.75 each, postage paid. 5 or more cards $2.50 each. Postage paid.

Overstreet Publications, 780 Hunt Cliff Dr. NW, Cleveland, TN 37311

GRADE: **MINT** (ONE - 100)

Example: Front cover of *Mad* #1, 1952. © E.C. Publ.
Obvious defects: None.
Hidden defects: None.
OWL: 9.

Note: This outstanding and rare example of an early 1950s comic book in Mint condition is from the famous "Gaines File Copy" collection.

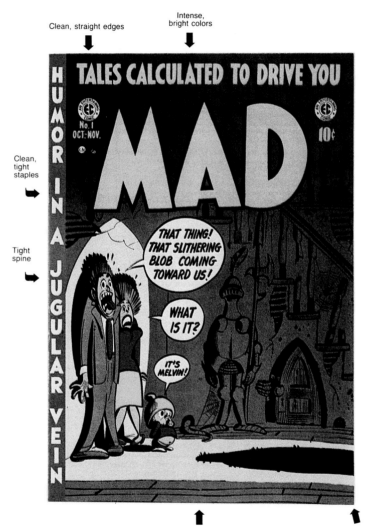

Clean, straight edges

Intense, bright colors

Clean, tight staples

Tight spine

A flat, perfect, flawless book

Perfect corners

GRADE: **MINT** (ONE - 99)

Example: Front cover of *All-American Comics* #16, 1940, © DC Comics.
Obvious defects: None.
Hidden defects: None.
OWL: 9.

Extremely light stress
line in circle

All edges are sharp

Tight
staple

Tight
spine

Tight
staple

Brilliant colors, square cut, flat and beautiful

Sharp corners

GRADE: **MINT** (ONE - **99**)

Example: Front cover of *Tales Of Suspense* #48, 1963. © Marvel Ent. Group.
Obvious defects: None.
Hidden defects: None.
OWL: 9.

Extremely slight
color fleck

Flat with
bright colors

Tight
spine

Cover surface
is flawless

Sharp corners

GRADE: **NEAR MINT** (ONE - 95)

Example: Front cover of *The Amazing Spider-Man* #1, 1963. © Marvel Ent. Group.
Obvious defects: None.
Hidden defects: None.
OWL: 9.

Note: This outstanding example is an unread newsstand copy purchased by the author. Its original condition was never any better.

GRADE: **NEAR MINT** (ONE - 94)

Example: Front cover of *Batman* #1, 1940. © DC Comics.
Obvious defects: None.
Hidden defects: None.
OWL: 8.

Note: This rare, outstanding copy ranks in the top five best known. Printing registration is excellent.

Sharp corners

Very slight foxing along edge

Tight staple

Tight spine

Tight staple

Light foxing

Brilliant colors

GRADE: **NEAR MINT** (ONE - 90)

Example: Front cover of *Speed Carter Spaceman* #1, 1953. © Marvel Ent. Group.
Obvious defects: None.
Hidden defects: None.
OWL: 8.

Very light edge wear   Pencilled check mark

Slight
edge
scrape

Tiny
edge
stress

Tight
staple

Tight
spine

Tight
staple

Tiny
color
fleck

Note: This copy is from the "White Mountain" collection.

GRADE: **VERY FINE** (ONE - 80)

Example: Front cover of *Silver Streak Comics* #7, 1941. © Lev Gleason.
Obvious defects: None.
Hidden defects: None.
OWL: 7.

Note: This book is very rare in this grade.

Light
staple
tear

Very
light
spine
stress
lines

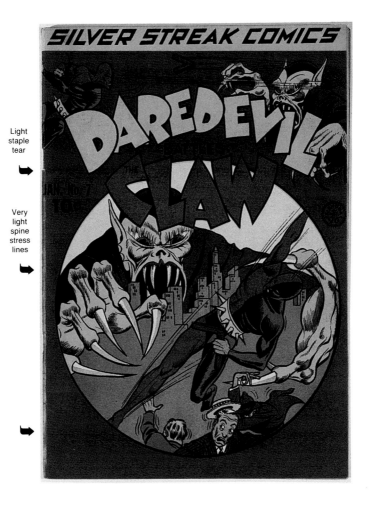

GRADE: **VERY FINE** (ONE - 78)

Example: Front cover of *Comic Cavalcade* #1, 1942. © DC Comics.
Obvious defects: None.
Hidden defects: None.
OWL: 7.

Note: This comic book is "square bound" with cardboard covers. Cover creasing and spine damage is commom on books of this type.

Very light corner abrasion

Light corner stain

Light reading crease

Color fleck

Excellent spine quality

Very light edge wear

GRADE: **VERY FINE** (ONE - **76**)

Example: Front cover of *Showcase* #22, 1959. © DC Comics.
Obvious defects: None.
Hidden defects: None.
OWL: 7.

Light corner abrasion

Tiny tear

Light corner crease

Staple stress lines

Light spine abrasion

Light spine stress lines

GRADE: **FINE** (ONE - 68)

Example: Front cover of *Fantastic Four* #1, 1961. © Marvel Ent. Group.
Obvious defects: None.
Hidden defects: None.
OWL: 8.

Very light staining along edge

Stress line

Transverse spine creases

Light corner crease

GRADE: **FINE** (ONE - 62)

Example: Front cover of *Showcase* #8, 1957. © DC Comics.
Obvious defects: None.
Hidden defects: None.
OWL: 6.

Light corner abrasion

Very light edge creasing

Very light corner crease

Staple stress lines

Small color scrape

Staple stress lines

Bindery defect 1a
(see glossary)

Light crease line

Very light corner crease

GRADE: **FINE** (ONE - 62)

Example: Front cover of *Green Giant Comics* #1, 1940. © Pelican Publ.
Obvious defects: None.
Hidden defects: None.
OWL: 7.

Color fleck

Light edge scrape

Light corner crease

Spine stress lines

Abraded edge

Light edge crease

Edge tear

GRADE: **VERY GOOD** (ONE - 46)

Example: Front cover of *Brave And The Bold* #30, 1960. © DC Comics.
Obvious defects: None.
Hidden defects: None.
OWL: 6.

Bindery defect 1a
(see glossary)

Edge crease

Rusty
staple

Transverse
spine
creases

Light
corner
crease

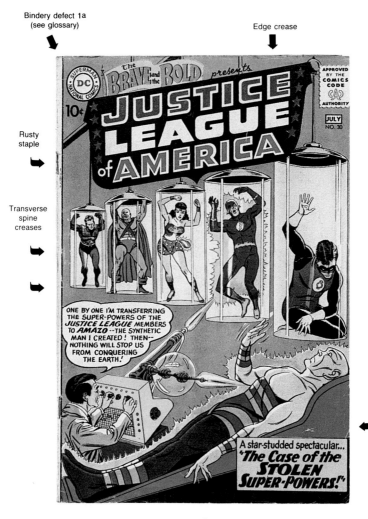

Cover has very light soiling and stress lines

GRADE: **VERY GOOD** (ONE - 42)

Example: Front cover of *Amazing Mystery Funnies* V2#8, 1939. © Centaur.
Obvious defects: Long corner crease.
Hidden defects: None.
OWL: 7.

Note: The long cover crease lowers the grade of this book from a Fine to Very Good.

Corner crease

Spine stress

Spine stress

Spine stress

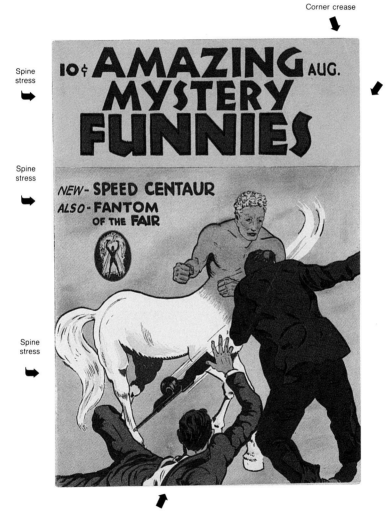

Long diagonal crease

GRADE: **VERY GOOD** (ONE - 40)

Example: Front cover of *Marvel Mystery Comics* #83, 1947. © Marvel Ent. Group.
Obvious defects: None.
Hidden defects: None.
OWL: 6.

Rolled spine

Multiple
vertical
reading
creases

Edge
tear

Edge
tear

Corner
crease

Store
stamp

Defect: Unobtrusive placement of store stamp does not affect grade. *My Friend Irma* #36, 1953. © Marvel Ent. Group.

Grease
pencil
arrival
date

Defect: Arrival date in grease pencil does not affect this grade. *Web Of Evil* #6, 1953. © Quality Comics.

Name
& initial
on cover

Small
corner
crease

Abraded corner

Abraded corner

Defect: Abraded corners. Grade before defect - VF87. Grade with defect - FN72. *Comic Cavalcade* #13, 1945. © DC Comics.

Light corner crease & stress line at top

Light crease along edge

Defect: Light cover creases. Grade before defect - VF85. Grade with defect - FN70. *Journey Into Mystery* #19, 1954. © Marvel Ent. Group.

Name in ink

Defect: Name on cover in ink. Light oxidation shadow at bottom. Grade before defect - VF83. Grade with defect - FN68. *Super Duck#9*, 1946. © Archie Publ.

Heavy grease pencil initial

Defect: Heavy grease pencil initial. Grade before defect - VF80. Grade with defect - FN68. *My Past Confessions #8*, 1949. © Fox Feat. Synd.

Dust shadow

Arrival date

Defect: Heavy dust shadow. Grade before defect - VF75. Grade with defect - FN65. *All Winners #6*, 1942. © Marvel Ent. Group.

Defect: Subscription label on front cover. Grade without label - VF82. Grade with label - FN65. *Walt Disney's C&S #153*, 1953. © Walt Disney Co.

Subscription label

Light corner crease

Defect: Corner crease. Grade before defect - VF87. Grade with defect - FN60. *Journey Into Mystery* #97, 1963. © Marvel Ent. Group.

Defect: "Complimentary" stamp on cover. Grade before defect - VF82. Grade with defect - FN56. *Down With Crime* #1, 1951. © Fawcett Publ.

Double cover stamp

Close up of
rat chew

Defect: Rat chew on right edge. Grade before defect - FN70. Grade with defect - FN 57. *Apache Kid* #13, 1955. © Marvel Ent. Group.

GRADE: VERY GOOD
Abbreviated Notation: VG

Overstreet Numerical Equivalent (ONE) range: 54-35
(**Highest** possible VG grade = 54, **Mid**-grade = 45, **Lowest** possible VG grade = 35)

GRADE DESCRIPTION:
The average used comic book. A comic in this grade shows moderate wear, can have a reading or center crease or a rolled spine, but still has not accumulated enough total defects to reduce eye appeal to the point where it is not a desirable copy. Some discoloration, fading and even minor soiling is allowed. No chunks (see glossary) can be missing but a small piece (see glossary) can be out at the corner or edge. Store stamps, name stamps, arrival dates, initials, etc. have no affect on this grade. Cover and interior pages can have minor tears and folds and the centerfold may be loose or detached. One or both staples might be loose, but cover is not completely detached. Common bindery and printing defects do not affect grade. Pages and inside covers may be brown but not brittle. Tape should never be used for comic book repair, however many VG condition comics have minor tape repair.

CHECKLIST FOR THE GRADE VERY GOOD:

- ✔ Shows significant wear.
- ✔ Book-length creases or dimples.
- ✔ Spine roll.
- ✔ Some discoloration, fading and soiling.
- ✔ Small piece can be out of cover from an otherwise finer copy.
- ✔ Store stamp, name stamp, arrival date, or initials.
- ✔ Staples may be discolored with rust migration.
- ✔ Centerfold may be detached.
- ✔ Minor printing and/or bindery defects.
- ✔ Pages may be brown.
- ✔ Minor tape repair on an otherwise better copy.

Note: Comics in this condition are desirable and collectible. The best known copies of some pre-1960 comic books are in Very Good condition.

Ⓐ **COLLECTOR ALERT:** There are significant and important differences between this grade and the next lower grade and overgrading sometimes occurs.

Ⓐ **COLLECTOR ALERT:** Comic books with brittle pages are not VG. When purchasing a comic suspected of being brittle, request the owner to open the book for examination.

Ⓐ **COLLECTOR ALERT:** Restored books often fall into this grade.

ACCUMULATED DEFECTS RULE:
Books in this grade will not have **all** the listed defects but will have a combination of some of the above defects. The final grade depends on the number and severity of defects listed under the checklist.

GRADE: **VERY GOOD** (ONE - 54)

Example: Front cover of *Showcase* # 23, 1959. © DC Comics.
Obvious defects: None.
Hidden defects: None.
OWL: 8.

Abraded corner

Light corner crease

Multiple transverse spine creases

Abraded corner

VERY GOOD (continued) - *Showcase*
Example: Front cover close ups.

Light corner crease

Tiny corner crease

Abraded corner

Multiple transverse spine creases

Abraded corner

Edge stress

Edge stress

Tiny corner crease

170

GRADE: **VERY GOOD** (ONE - 48)

Example: Front cover of *Challengers Of The Unknown* #4, 1958. © DC Comics.
Obvious defects: None.
Hidden defects: Centerfold detached from lower staple. Upper staple completely discolored. Printing out-of-register on interior two pages.
OWL: 5.

Rounded corner

Ragged edge due to
over-cover (see glossary)

Rounded corner

Abraded
spine
area

Staple
stress

Transverse
spine
creases

Minor rounded corner

Small multiple
corner creases

172

Light corner crease

Ragged edge due to over-cover (see glossary)

Abraded corner

Abraded spine

Edge tear

Corner crease

Minor center crease

Abraded corner

GRADE: **VERY GOOD** (ONE - 46)

Example: Front cover of *Forbidden Worlds* #82, 1959. © American Comics Group.
Obvious defects: None.
Hidden defects: None.
OWL: 6.

Abraded corner

Slight ragged edge
due to over-cover

Small
corner
crease

Transverse
creases
on spine

Minor
soiling

Water
stain

Edge
stress
line

Double
corner
creases

VERY GOOD (continued) - *Forbidden Worlds*
Example: Front cover close ups.

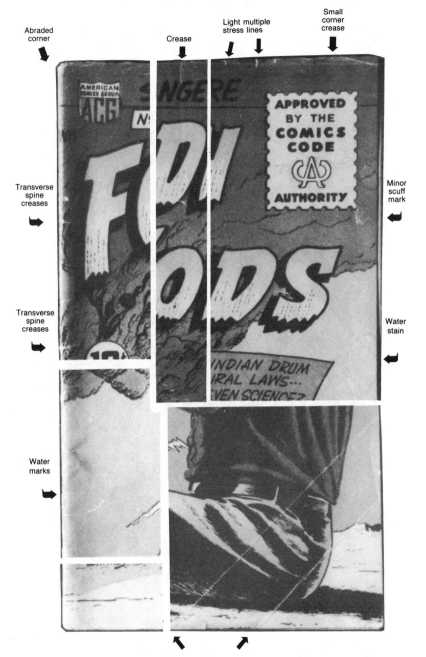

Abraded corner

Crease

Light multiple stress lines

Small corner crease

Transverse spine creases

Minor scuff mark

Transverse spine creases

Water stain

Water marks

Double corner creases

GRADE: **VERY GOOD** (ONE - 45)

Example: Front cover of *Action Comics* #47, 1942. © DC Comics.
Obvious defects: None.
Hidden defects: None.
OWL: 7.

Rolled spine

Color flecks

Light corner crease

Initial and date stamp

Staple tear

Edge wear

Color flecks

Light corner crease

Fanned pages due to spine roll

Crease

Book-length oxidation shadow

Long crease

Sun shadow along bottom edge

Glued tear

Oxidation shadow along spine

GRADE: **VERY GOOD** (ONE - 45)

Example: Front cover of *Marvel Tales* #93, 1949. © Marvel Ent. Group.
Obvious defects: Dust shadow.
Hidden defects: Severe staple tears, but cover is still attached.
OWL: 5.

Light dust shadow along top edge

Book-length dust shadow

Severe staple tears

Pencil initial

Foxing

Severe staple tears

Grease pencil initial

Small tear

Book-length dust shadow

GRADE: **VERY GOOD** (ONE - 45)

Example: Front cover of *Detective Comics* #316, 1963. © DC Comics.
Obvious defects: None.
Hidden defects: Name written in ball point pen on page 1. First and second center-fold detached at bottom staple.
OWL: 6.

Slight rolled spine

Long light corner crease

Long crease

Spine stress

Minor cover dents

Color scrape

Enlarged staple hole

Abraded corner

Impacted corner

GRADE: **VERY GOOD** (ONE - 43)

Example: Front cover of *Detective Comics* #4, 1937. © DC Comics.
Obvious defects: None.
Hidden defects: Two inch tear in 4 interior pages. Centerfold completely detached.
OWL: 5.

Slight rolled spine

Light, book-length crease

Minor color fleck

Long crease

Minor discoloration

Very minor corner crease

Small staple tears

Loose staple

Very minor edge tears

Minor corner tear

Light soiling and wrinkling over entire cover

Light corner crease

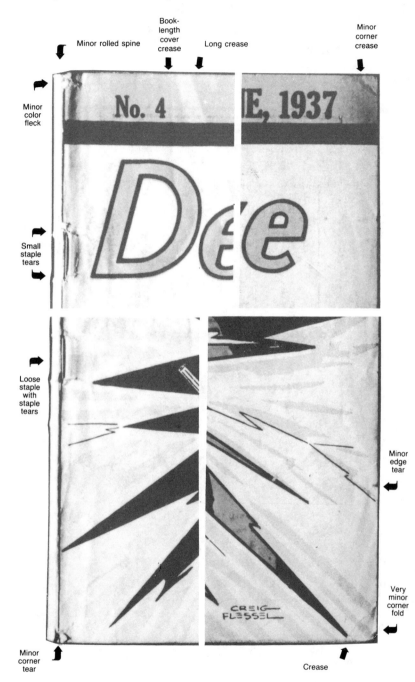

Minor rolled spine

Book-length cover crease

Long crease

Minor corner crease

Minor color fleck

No. 4

E, 1937

Small staple tears

Loose staple with staple tears

Minor edge tear

Very minor corner fold

CREIG FLESSEL

Minor corner tear

Crease

182

GRADE: **VERY GOOD** (ONE - 42)

Example: Front cover of *Detective Comics* #225, 1956. © DC Comics.
Obvious defects: None.
Hidden defects: None.
OWL: 6.

Multiple creases

Rat chew

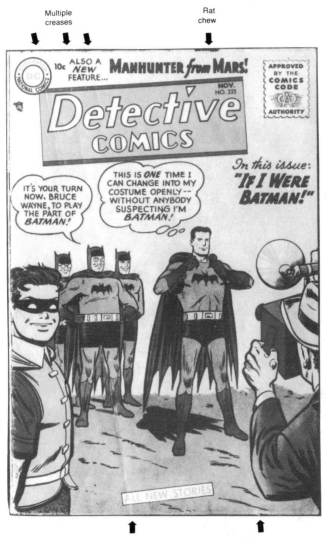

Long crease

Small rat chew

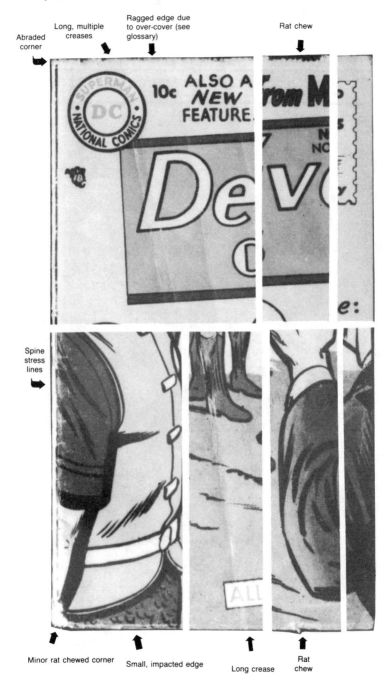

Abraded corner

Long, multiple creases

Ragged edge due to over-cover (see glossary)

Rat chew

Spine stress lines

Minor rat chewed corner

Small, impacted edge

Long crease

Rat chew

GRADE: **VERY GOOD** (ONE - 40)

Example: Front cover of *The Flame* #1, 1940. © Fox Feat. Synd.
Obvious defects: Rolled spine.
Hidden defects: 1'' tear on two inside pages.
OWL: 6.

Rolled spine   Edge tear   Long, light crease

Staple tears

Spine tear

Staple tears

Color scrape

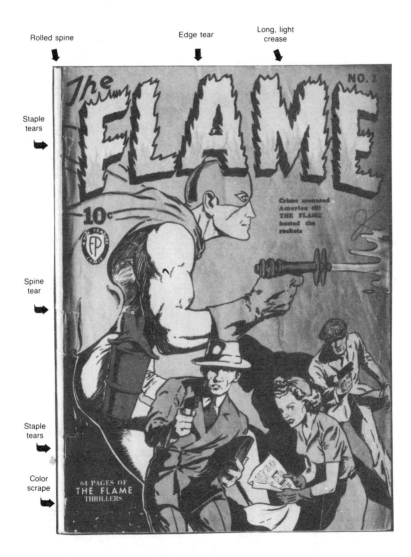

Rolled spine

Tiny corner crease

Glued
staple
tear

Spine
stess
lines

Staple
tear

Long
light
corner
crease

Color
fleck

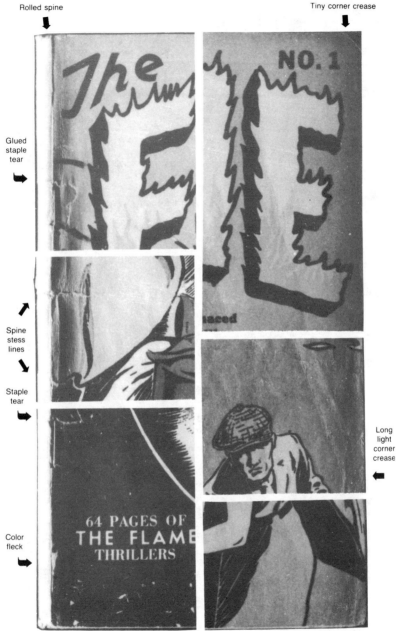

64 PAGES OF
THE FLAME
THRILLERS

GRADE: **VERY GOOD** (ONE - 40)

Example: Front cover of *The Fantastic Four* #3, 1962. © Marvel Ent. Group.
Obvious defects: None.
Hidden defects: Centerfold loose at upper staple.
OWL: 6.

Progressive spine roll
(most pronounced at top)

Water
stain

Cover edges offset (fanned)
due to rolled spine

Staple
tear

Edge
tear

Minor
stain

Multiple
transverse
spine
creases

Edge
chips

Book-
length
reading
crease

Minor
corner
blunting

Minor edge wear

Minor
corner
crease

VERY GOOD (continued) - *The Fantastic Four*
Example: Front cover close ups.

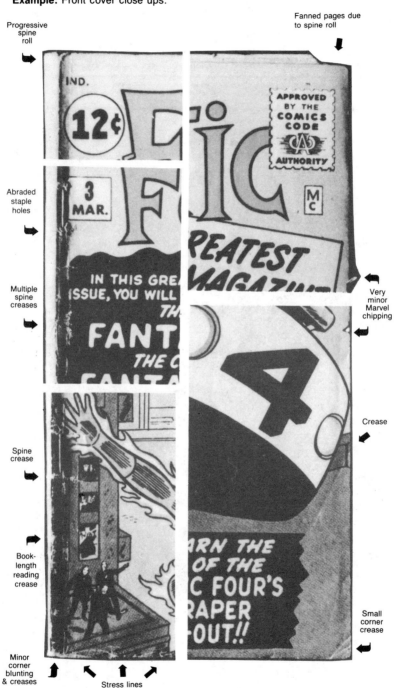

Progressive spine roll

Fanned pages due to spine roll

Abraded staple holes

Multiple spine creases

Very minor Marvel chipping

Spine crease

Crease

Book-length reading crease

Minor corner blunting & creases

Stress lines

Small corner crease

GRADE: **VERY GOOD** (ONE - 36)

Example: Front cover of *Amazing Mystery Funnies* #1, 1938. © Centaur Publ.
Obvious defects: None.
Hidden defects: None.
OWL: 6.

Small
color
scrape

Corner crease

Staple
tears

Spine
stress

1'' glued
spine
split

Cover wrinkling

Corner crease

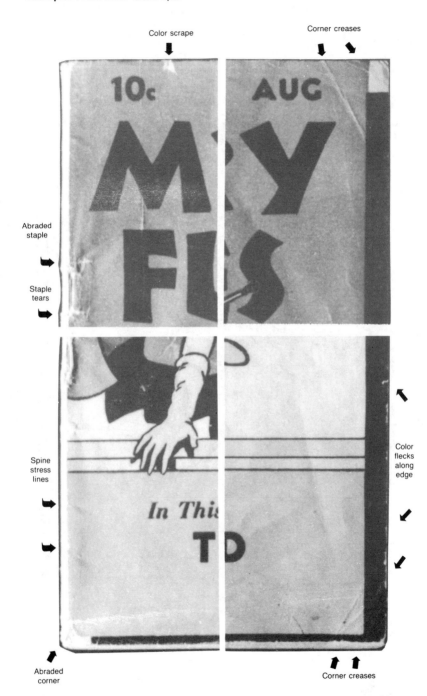

Color scrape

Corner creases

Abraded
staple

Staple
tears

Spine
stress
lines

Color
flecks
along
edge

In This

TO

Abraded
corner

Corner creases

GRADE: **VERY GOOD** (ONE - 36)

Example: Front cover of *Action Comics* #4, 1938. © DC Comics.
Obvious defects: Book length cover fold.
Hidden defects: Corner folding on some interior pages.
OWL: 8.

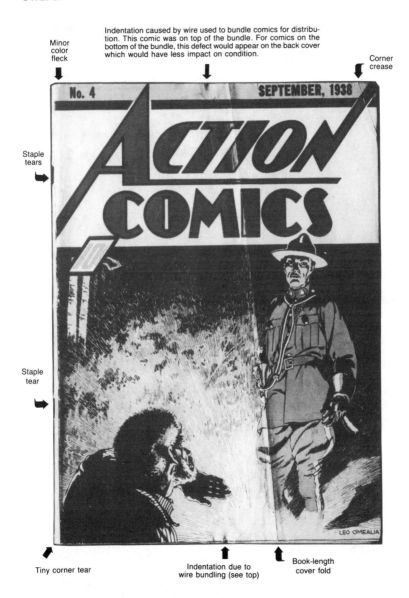

Minor color fleck

Indentation caused by wire used to bundle comics for distribution. This comic was on top of the bundle. For comics on the bottom of the bundle, this defect would appear on the back cover which would have less impact on condition.

Corner crease

Staple tears

Staple tear

Tiny corner tear

Indentation due to wire bundling (see top)

Book-length cover fold

Note: Books of this age rarely have such a high Overstreet Whiteness Level. This factor increases the grade (ONE) of this comic book. Seasoned collectors place great importance on the whiteness of the interior cover and pages.

VERY GOOD (continued) - *Action Comics*
Example: Front cover close ups.

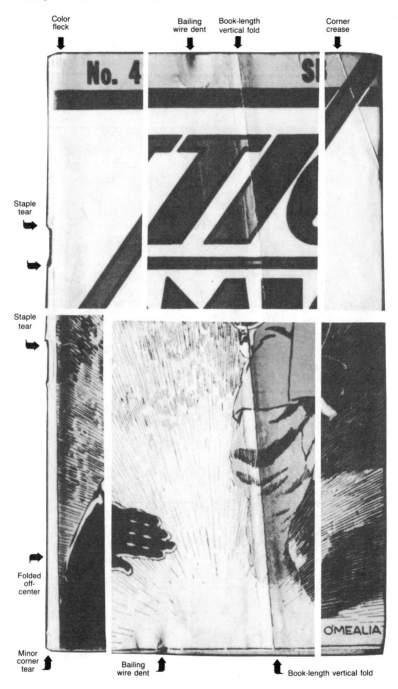

Color fleck

Bailing wire dent

Book-length vertical fold

Corner crease

Staple tear

Staple tear

No. 4

SI

Folded off-center

Minor corner tear

Bailing wire dent

Book-length vertical fold

O'MEALIA

GRADE: **VERY GOOD** (ONE - 36)

Example: Front cover of *Dale Evans* #1, 1948. © DC Comics.
Obvious defects: Rolled spine.
Hidden defects: Detached centerfold.
OWL: 6.

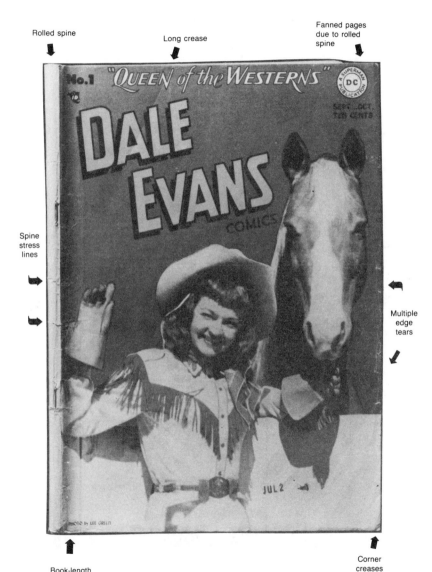

Rolled spine

Long crease

Fanned pages due to rolled spine

Spine stress lines

Multiple edge tears

Book-length fading

Corner creases

GRADE: **VERY GOOD** (ONE - 35)

Example: Front cover of *America's Greatest Comics* #3, 1942. © Fawcett Publ.
Obvious defects: None.
Hidden defects: First and second page are torn at binding.
OWL: 6.

Minor bindery corner

Edge stress creases

Numerous corner creases

Blunted corner

Transverse stress line

Multiple creases in center of book

Book-length reading crease, typical of square bound books

Abraded corner

Minor
bindery
corner

Multiple corner
creases

Blunted
corner

Transverse
stress
line

Book-
length
reading
crease

Small
color
flecks

Stress lines

Abraded corner

Stress
lines

Small stress lines

Book-length cover creases

Corner tear

Color scrape

Stress lines

Corner tear

Book-length cover creases

GRADE: VERY GOOD
DEFECT SECTION

The grade of all of the books in this section have (a) dropped from either a higher grade to the Very Good grade due to a specific damaging defect, or (b) have dropped a few points within this grade.

Heavy grease pencil initial & date stamp

Defect: Heavy grease pencil initial and date stamp on cover does not affect this grade. *Star Spangled Comics* #12, 1942. © DC Comics.

Defect: Light foxing and pencilled name and date on cover which does not affect this grade. *Suzie* #53, 1946. © Archie Comics.

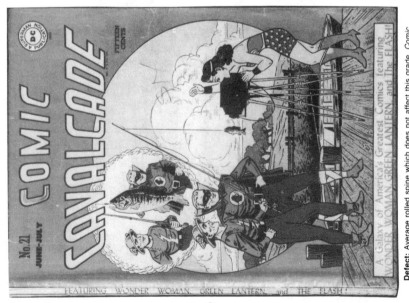

Defect: Average rolled spine which does not affect this grade. *Comic Cavalcade* #21, 1947. © DC Comics.

Store stamp

Defect: Store stamp and bindery defect does not affect this grade. *Real Screen Comics* #34, 1951. © DC Comics.

Long vertical printing crease near center of book

Defect: Book length vertical printing crease which does not affect this grade. *Rocket Ship X* #1, 1951. © Fox Feat. Synd.

Name in pencil

Name initial in grease pencil

Defect: Two name initials on cover, one in grease pencil. Grade before defect - FN65. Grade with defect - VG52. *Police Comics #44*, 1945. © Quality Comics.

Glued split spine

Defect: Glued two inch spine split. Grade before defect - FN65. Grade with defect - VG50. *Daring Mystery Comics #8*, 1942. © Marvel Ent. Group.

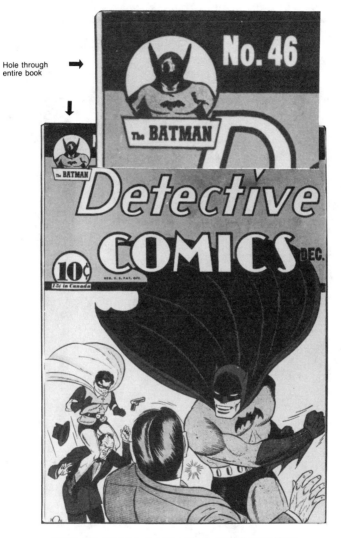

Hole through
entire book

Defect: Hole drilled through entire comic at upper left corner. Grade
before defect - VF80. Grade with defect - VG50. *Detective Comics* #45,
1940. © DC Comics.

File
Copy
stamp

Defect: Comic producer cover stamp, brown pages (OWL2). Grade before defect - VF85. Grade with defect - VG50. *Star Spangled Comics* #54, 1946. © DC Comics.

Long
light
corner
crease

Defect: Long cover crease and bindery trim, type 2c (see glossary). Grade before defect - VF85. Grade with defect - VG50. *Ace Comics* #118, 1947. © King Feat. Synd.

Light subscription crease at center of book

Defect: Light subscription center crease on front cover. Back cover subscription label does not affect this grade. Grade before defect - FN65. Grade with defect - VG48. *Walt Disney's C&S #76*, 1947. © Walt Disney Co.

Letters filled in with pencil

Defect: Letters in circle have been filled in with pencil. Grade before defect - FN60. Grade with defect - VG48. *Star Spangled Comics* #10, 1942. © DC Comics.

Large grease pencil price mark

Defect: Large grease pencil price on cover. Grade before defect - FN65. Grade with defect - VG45. *Star Ranger Funnies V2#5*, 1939. © Centaur Publ.

Very large name stamp

Defect: Large name stamp and light center crease on cover. Grade before defect - FN65. Grade with defect - VG45. *Sensation Comics* #35, 1944. © DC Comics.

Edge re-trimmed at top and on right side

Bottom not trimmed

Defect: Book was re-trimmed at top and on right side. Grade before defect - VF82. Grade with defect - VG45. *All Star Comics* #24, 1945. © DC Comics.

Date stamp

Erased
check
mark

Inside
pages
are
brown

Defect: Brown pages (Owl2), erased check mark and date stamp. Grade before defect - VF80. Grade with defect - VG45. *Smash Comics #67*, 1946. © Quality Comics.

Minor
water
damage
at
corner

Defect: Minor water damage on upper left corner. Grade before defect - FN65. Grade with defect - VG45. *True Complete Mystery #7*, 1949. © Marvel Ent. Group.

Rusty
staple

Rusty
staple

Defect: Heavily rusted staples with rust penetrating to centerfold. Grade before defect - FN65. Grade with defect VG45. *Mysterious Adventures* #10, 1952. © Story Comics.

Circled
name
stamp

Defect: Name stamp on cover that is circled in ink. Grade before defect - FN65. Grade with defect - VG45. *Boy Loves Girl* #27, 1952. © Lev Gleason.

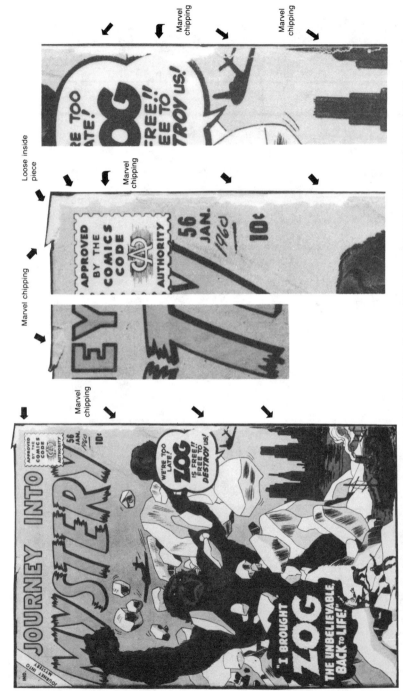

Defects: Marvel chipping along edges. Grade before defect - VF88. Grade with defect - VG45. "Marvel chipping" is a bindery defect caused by a dull paper trimmer and/or improper clamping of the paper in the cutter. This defect is very common in Marvels of the 1950s and 60s. *Journey Into Mystery* #56, 1960. © Marvel Ent. Group.

Loose staple

Defect: Loose staple. Grade before defect - FN65. Grade with defect - VG45. *Superman* #169, 1964. © DC Comics.

Mis-trimmed

Defect: Severe bindery cutting defect, type 2c (See glossary). Grade before defect - VF85. Grade with defect - VG45. *The Advs. Of Superman* #475, 1991. © DC Comics.

Corner crease

Defect: Long corner crease. Grade before defect - VG48. Grade with defect - VG42. *Mysterious Suspense #1*, 1958. © Charlton Comics.

Light center crease

Subscription label on front cover

Note: Cover art was designed to accomodate subscription label/stamp.

Defect: Subscription label and light crease on front cover. Grade without defects - FN65. Grade with defects - VG40. *Walt Disney's C&S #149*, 1953. © Walt Disney Co.

Smoke damage along spine

Smoke damage

Defect: Smoke damage on back cover. Grade before defect - FN65. Grade with defect - VG40. **Note:** As a general rule, defects on the back cover have much less impact on grade than defects on the front cover. *Star Comics* V2#6, 1939. © Centaur Publ.

Defect: Restaple holes completely through book at spine. Grade before defect - VG50. Grade with defect - VG38. *Star Spangled Comics* #1, 1941. © DC Comics.

Double staple holes

Double staple holes

Corner piece missing

Defect: Corner piece is missing. Grade before defect - FN65. Grade with defect - VG37. *Sensation Comics* #62, 1947. © DC Comics.

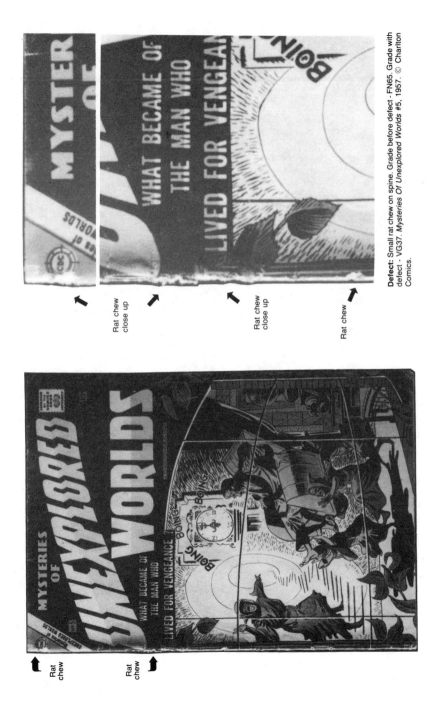

Rat chew close up

Rat chew close up

Rat chew

Rat chew

Rat chew

Defect: Small rat chew on spine. Grade before defect - FN65. Grade with defect - VG37. *Mysteries Of Unexplored Worlds* #5, 1957. © Charlton Comics.

Large publishers stamp in obtrusive location

Smoke damage

Defect: Large publishers stamp in an obtrusive location. Grade before defect - VG40. Grade with defect - VG36. *Mickey Mouse Mag. #7,* 1936. © The Walt Disney Co.

Defect: Smoke damage along spine and across lower cover. Grade before defect - FN70. Grade with defect - VG36. *Amazing Mystery Funnies #3,* 1938. © Centaur Publ.

Smoke damage

Smoke damage

Smoke damage

214

Ink in logo

Store stamp

Defect: Inked tracing in center of logo. Grade before defect - VF80. Grade with defect - VG36. *Doll Man Quarterly #12*, 1947. © Quality Comics.

Long tape repair

Off-center staple

Tape

Defect: Taped spine and store stamp. Grade before defect - FN65. Grade with defect - VG35. *Star Comics V2#7*, 1939. © Centaur Publ.

GRADE: GOOD
Abbreviated Notation: GD

Overstreet Numerical Equivalent (ONE) range: 34-15
(**Highest** possible GD grade = 34, **Mid**-grade = 25, **Lowest** possible GD grade = 15)

GRADE DESCRIPTION:
A copy in this grade has all pages and its cover, although there may be small pieces missing. Books in this grade are commonly creased, scuffed, abraded and soiled, but are completely readable. Often paper quality may be low but not brittle. Cover reflectivity is usually low and in some cases completely absent. Most collectors consider this the lowest collectible grade because comic books in lesser condition are often incomplete and/or brittle. Traditionally, collectors have sometimes found it difficult to differentiate this grade from the next lower grade. This task can be simplified if one remembers that a comic book in this condition can have a large accumulation of defects *but still maintains its basic structural integrity.*

CHECKLIST FOR THE GRADE GOOD:

- ✓ Shows substantial wear.
- ✓ Must be readable.
- ✓ Discoloration, fading and soiling likely.
- ✓ Small pieces may be missing, but the readability is preserved.
- ✓ Store stamp, name stamp, arrival date, initials permitted.
- ✓ Staples may be degraded, absent, or replaced.
- ✓ Cover may be detached.
- ✓ Coupon may be cut from back cover or from an interior page as long as story readability is preserved.
- ✓ Pages may be brown but not brittle.
- ✓ Tape and other forms of repair are common.

Note: Some of the most collectible comic books are rarely found in better than Good condition.

☒ **COLLECTOR ALERT:** A book with brittle edges can be kept in this condition if handled carefully. However, its life expectancy is short.

☒ **COLLECTOR ALERT:** The lowest price listed in the Price Guide is for Good condition comic books, and some have found it expedient to over-grade in an attempt to justify this price.

☒ **COLLECTOR ALERT:** Comic books with brittle pages are not in GD condition.

ACCUMULATED DEFECTS RULE:
Books in this grade will not have **all** the listed defects but will have a combination of some of the above defects. The final grade depends on the number and severity of defects listed under the checklist.

GRADE: **GOOD** (ONE - **34**)

Example: Front cover of *Funny Picture Stores* #2, 1936. © Comics Magazine.
Obvious defects: None.
Hidden defects: Light corner fold, first 4 pages. Small coffee stain, 1 page.
OWL: 7.

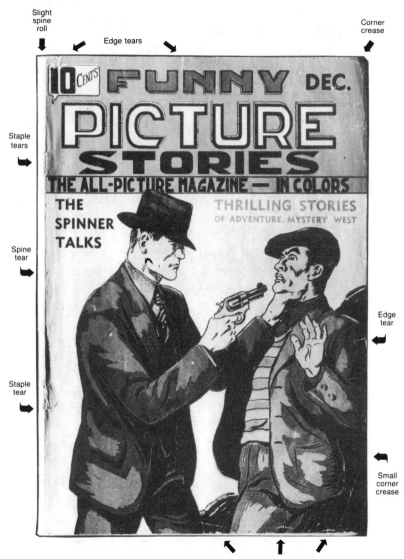

Slight spine roll

Edge tears

Corner crease

Staple tears

Spine tear

Staple tear

Edge tear

Small corner crease

Stress marks

Rolled spine

Light edge tears

Corner crease

Staple tears

Edge tear

Color flecks and cover dents

Staple tear

Small piece out

Edge stress

Multiple corner creases

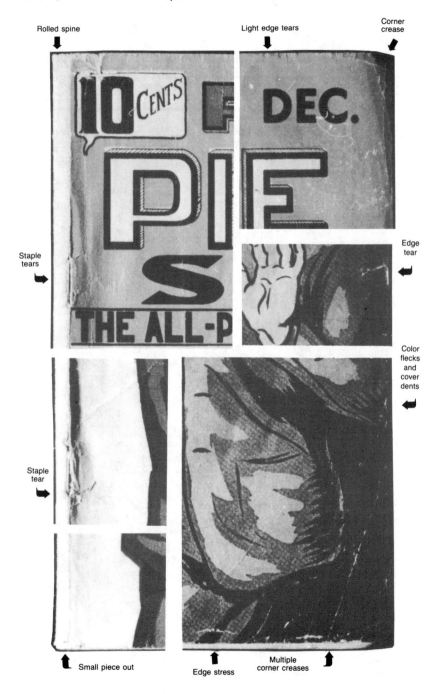

Corner creases

Edge
tear

Spine
tear

Fanned pages
due to rolled spine

Corner creases

GRADE: **GOOD** (ONE - **33**)

Example: Front cover of *Zip-Jet* #1, 1953. © St. John Publ.
Obvious defects: None.
Hidden defects: None.
OWL: 7.

Abraded corner

Edge creases

Minor corner crease

Spine creases

Crease

Smeared date stamp

Minor transverse spine creases

Corner crease

Bindery defect type 1a

Minor corner crease

Minor corner crease

Corner crease

Book-length crease

Impacted corner

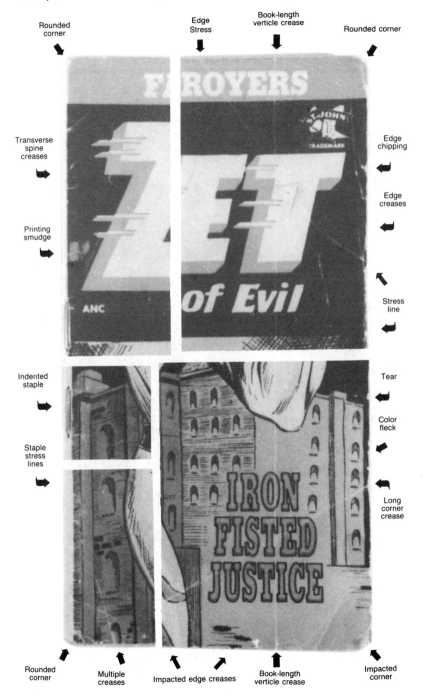

Rounded corner

Edge Stress

Book-length verticle crease

Rounded corner

Transverse spine creases

Edge chipping

Edge creases

Printing smudge

Stress line

Indented staple

Tear

Color fleck

Staple stress lines

Long corner crease

Rounded corner

Multiple creases

Impacted edge creases

Book-length verticle crease

Impacted corner

GRADE: **GOOD** (ONE - 30)

Example: Front cover of *Marvel Mystery Comics* #11, 1940. © Marvel Ent. Group.
Obvious defects: Long cover creases.
Hidden defects: Corners folded on several inside pages.
OWL: 5.

Note: The long cover creases drop the grade of this book from a VG45 to GD30. Colors are bright and the cover is clean.

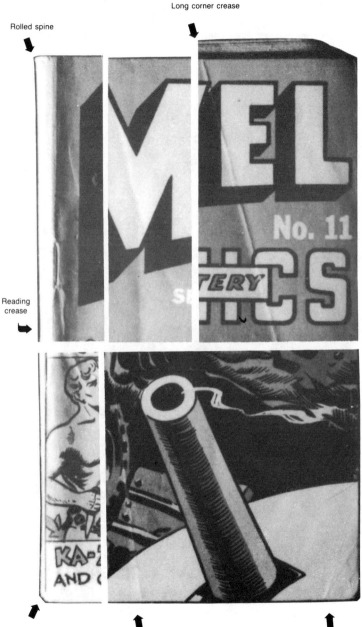

Long corner crease

Rolled spine

Reading crease

Bindery corner

Reading crease

Corner crease

GRADE: **GOOD** (ONE - **30**)

Example: Front cover of *Tarzan* #16, 1950. © ERB.
Obvious defects: None.
Hidden defects: Staples are rusty. Rust stains migrated into the paper to the centerfold.
OWL: 4.

Color flake

Color flake

Rusty staple

Multiple Transverse creases

Multiple stratified vertical creases

Rusty staple

Light stress mark

Color scrape

Long crease

Blunted corner

GRADE: **GOOD** (ONE - 30)

Example: Front cover of *My Greatest Adventure* #40, 1960. © DC Comics.
Obvious defects: Water damage to upper left corner.
Hidden defects: Two centerfolds detached. Water damage on upper corner of
interior pages of entire book.
OWL: 4.

Abraded corner

Long crease

Ragged edge due to over-cover

Corner crease

Large water mark

Rusty staple

Spine stress

Stress line

Abraded corner

Long crease

Abraded corner

GRADE: **GOOD** (ONE - **25**)

Example: Front cover of *Fantasy Masterpieces* #7, 1967. © Marvel Ent. Group.
Obvious defects: Torn corner.
Hidden defects: Multiple corner folds on interior pages. Several pages with small margin tears. Rusty staples.
OWL: 5.

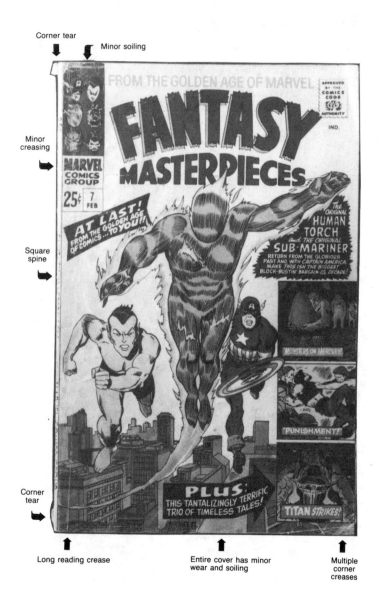

Corner tear

Minor soiling

Minor creasing

Square spine

Corner tear

Long reading crease

Entire cover has minor wear and soiling

Multiple corner creases

Corner crease

Corner tear

Staple ridge

Note hole caused by staple penetration with rust stain

Contraction/shrinkage along spine-typical of square bound comics.

Minor soiling

Staple ridge

Note hole caused by staple penetration with rust stain

Long corner crease

Impacted edge

Corner crease

Corner tear

GRADE: **GOOD** (ONE - 22)

Example: Front cover of *World's Finest Comics* #113, 1960. © DC Comics.
Obvious defects: Fanned pages at top. Tear at bottom of spine.
Hidden defects: Centerfold loose. Tears in margins of interior pages.
OWL: 5.

Progressive spine roll

Tear

Spine tear

NOV. NO. 113

APPROVED BY THE COMICS CODE AUTHORITY

Loose staple with piece out

POP!

Tear

Color fleck

1" spine tear

Abraded corner

Small, multiple edge tears

Edge wear

Corner crease

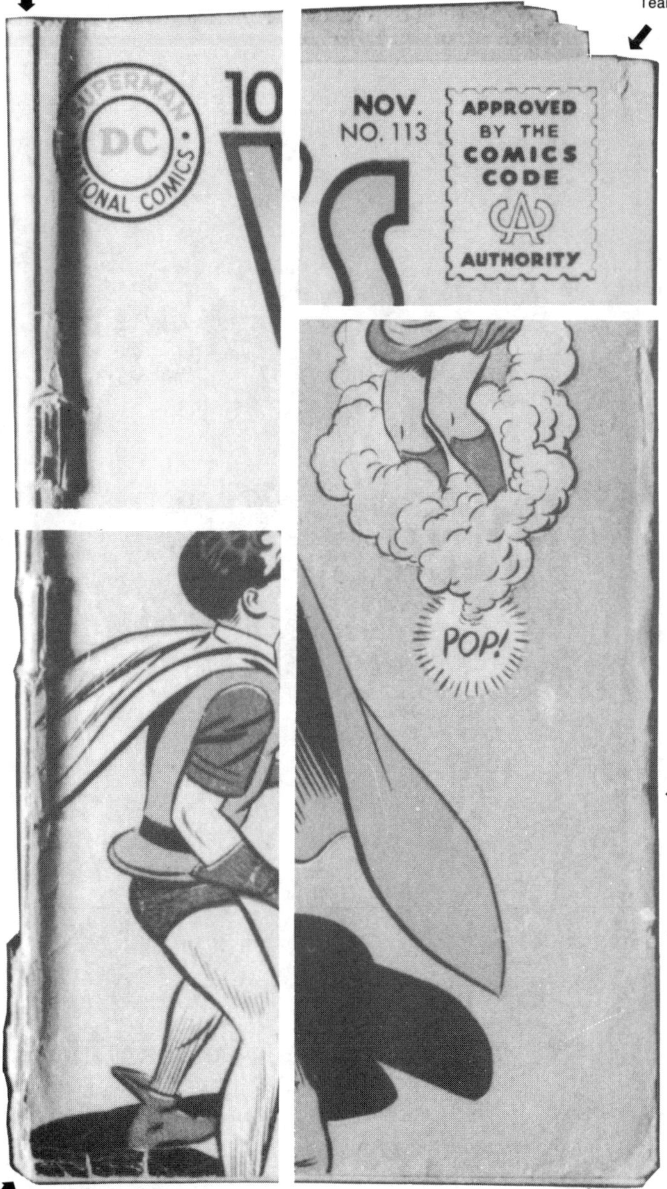

GRADE: **GOOD** (ONE - 20)

Example: Front cover of *New Comics* #11, 1936. © DC Comics.
Obvious defects: Heavily wrinkled and stained from water damage.
Hidden defects: Centerfold loose. Inside pages are wrinkled.
OWL: 4.

Abraded corner

Long corner crease

Transverse spine creases

Water stain

Transverse spine creases

Abraded corner

Extremely wrinkled and wavy cover due to water damage

Long crease

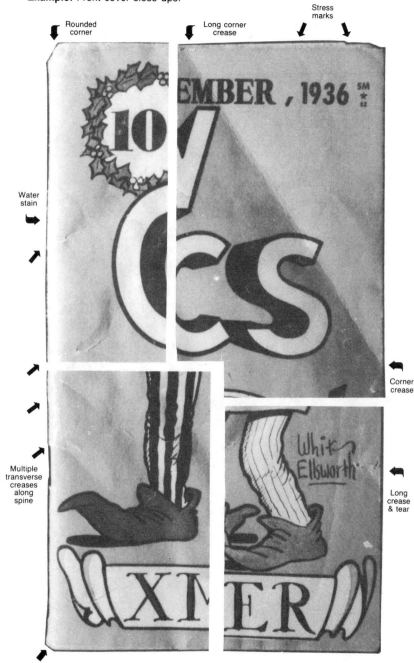

GRADE: **GOOD** (ONE - 20)

Example: Front cover of *Doll Man Quarterly* #2, 1942. © Quality Comics.
Obvious defects: Ragged spine.
Hidden defects: Numerous holes along inside spine and glued piece of cover at lower
  staple. Significant browning on inside covers.
OWL: 5 to 6.

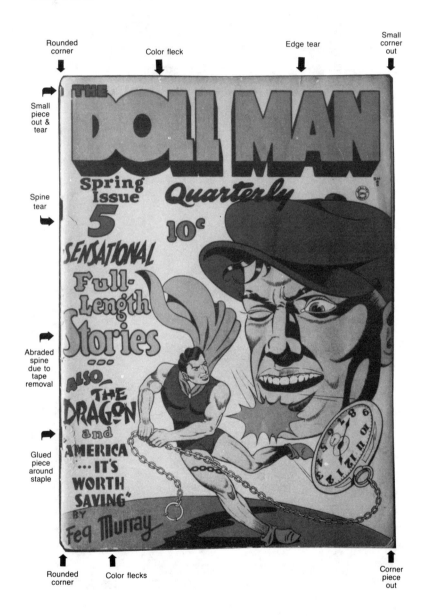

Rounded
corner

Color fleck

Edge tear

Small
corner
out

Small
piece
out &
tear

Spine
tear

Abraded
spine
due to
tape
removal

Glued
piece
around
staple

Rounded
corner

Color flecks

Corner
piece
out

Rounded corner

Edge tear

Rounded corner & small piece out

Piece out & tear

Staple tear

Staple tears

Glued spine split & piece around staple

Abraded spine due to tape removal

Heavily abraded corner

Color flecks

Corner piece out

GRADE: **GOOD** (ONE - 18)

Example: Front cover of *Feature Funnies* #3, 1937. © Quality Comics.
Obvious defects: Split spine and soiling on cover.
Hidden defects: Inside spine completely split and taped.
OWL: 4.

Corner cover piece out

Tear

Corner crease

Transverse spine tears

Transverse spine tears

Multiple edge tears

Book-length tape on inside spine

Edge tear   Edge tear

Rounded corner & crease

Corner piece out

Tear

Edge tear

Corner crease

Long tear

Spine stress lines

Book-length spine tape from inside

Many tears on right edge

Book-length tape on inside spine

Edge tear

Rounded corner and crease

GRADE: **GOOD** (ONE - 18)

Example: Front cover of *Giant Comics Editions* #11 (Western Picture Stories), 1949.
© St. John.
Obvious defects: Heavy creases and taped spine corners.
Hidden defects: Interior pages are severely bent and folded at corners through
entire book.
OWL: 4.

Note: This square bound comic, like most square bounds of the late 1940s and early
1950s, consists of rebound remainders (see glossary). This particular issue contains
four 32 page coverless comic books and a new cover.

Edge tear

Multiple spine creases

Tear

Transfer rust stain from staple of another book

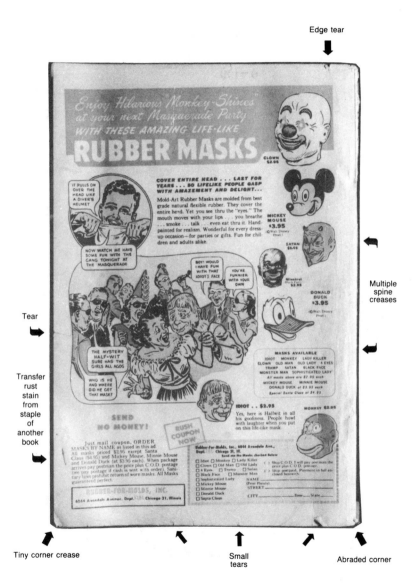

Tiny corner crease

Small tears

Abraded corner

GRADE: **GOOD** (ONE - **17**)

Example: Front cover of *Hopalong Cassidy* #3, 1946. © Fawcett Publ.
Obvious defects: Loose staple and rip through entire book.
Hidden defects: Loose centerfold. 3'' rip across first page.
OWL: 6.

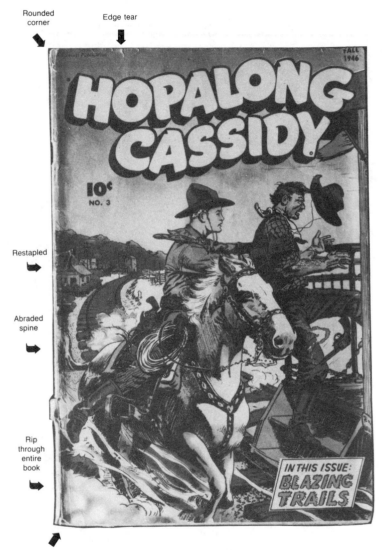

Rounded corner

Edge tear

Restapled

Abraded spine

Rip through entire book

Spine tear

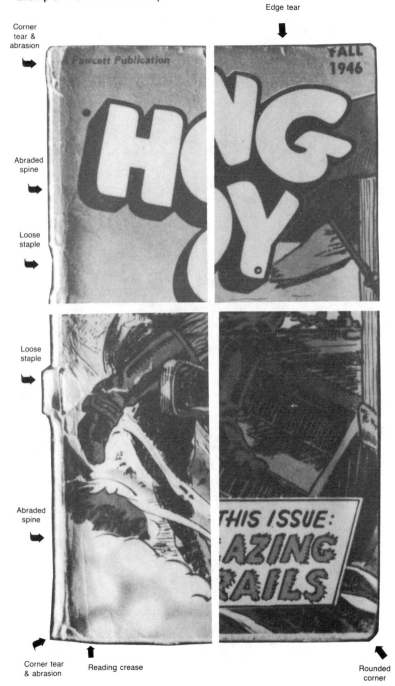

Edge tear

Corner
tear &
abrasion

Abraded
spine

Loose
staple

Loose
staple

Abraded
spine

Corner tear   Reading crease
& abrasion

Rounded
corner

GRADE: **GOOD** (ONE - **17**)

Example: Front cover of *Manhunt* #14 (A-1 #77), 1953. © Magazine Ent.
Obvious defects: Insect damage penetrating entire book at bottom.
Hidden defects: None.
OWL: 6.

Note: Without the insect damage, this book would grade VG50. The damage is in an unobtrusive location that does not affect the story or the central cover art.

Close up: Note three holes, two of which penetrate entire book.

GRADE: **GOOD** (ONE - 16)

Example: Front cover of *Adventure Comics* #218, 1955. © DC Comics.
Obvious defects: Heavily abraded and faded cover.
Hidden defects: Soiled inside pages. Some interior pages are torn, others are stained and/or folded at corners. Lower staple is rusty.
OWL: 4.

GOOD (continued) - *Adventure Comics*
Example: Front cover close ups.

Abraded corner

Small pieces out

Long corner creases & edge tear

Multiple transverse spine creases

Heavy abraded spine

Abraded corner

Abraded edge

Multiple corner creases

GRADE: **GOOD** (ONE - 15)

Example: Front cover of *King Comics* #3, 1936. © King Feat. Synd.
Obvious defects: Long spine split.
Hidden defects: Cover is completely detached. Crayon in margins of some interior
pages. Sun shadow on first page edge.
OWL: 5.

Slight progressive
spine roll

Edge tears

Check
mark

Bindery
corner

Spine
split

Tear

Loose
staple

Transverse
spine
tears

Loose
staple

Long
spine
split

Cover is loose from book

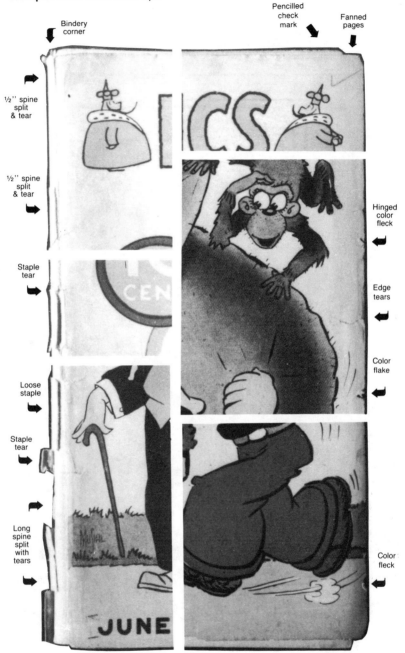

GRADE: **GOOD** (ONE - 15)

Example: Front cover of *Tarzan* #15, 1950. © ERB.

Obvious defects: Ragged spine, exposed pages along right edge indicating cover is detached.

Hidden defects: Cover is completely detached. Rusty staples and rust stains to centerfold. Multiple folded corners on interior pages.

OWL: 4 to 5.

Rolled spine

Light corner crease

Loose staple

Color flecks

Paper missing at staple

Multiple corner creases

Shifted cover due to loose staples

Corner creases

GOOD (continued) - *Tarzan*
Example: Front cover close ups.

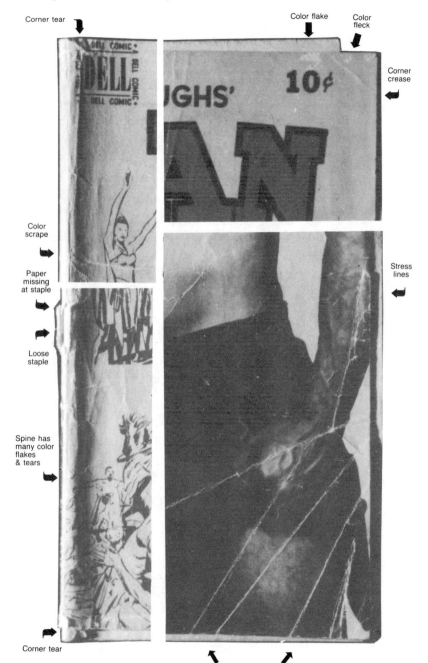

Corner tear

Color flake

Color fleck

Corner crease

Color scrape

Paper missing at staple

Loose staple

Spine has many color flakes & tears

Stress lines

Corner tear

Multiple corner creases

GRADE: GOOD
DEFECT SECTION

The grade of all of the books in this section have (a) dropped from either a higher grade to the Good grade due to a specific damaging defect, or (b) have dropped a few points within this grade.

Corner crease

Defect: Water damage over 60% of book, stains, and long cover crease. This example is from the "Lamont Larson" collection. Grade before defect - VF82. Grade with defect - GD25. *Adventure Comics* #33, 1938. © DC Comics.

Water stains & damage

Heavy writing on cover ⬆

Defect: Heavy writing on cover. Grade before defect - VG40. Grade with defect - GD25. *Famous Funnies #22*, 1936. © Eastern Color.

Tape ⬆

Tape ⬆

Tape ⬆

Defect: Tape on spine. Grade before defect - FN65. Grade with defect - GD25. *Target Comics V2#4*, 1941. © Novelty Press.

Center crease

Defect: Heavy subscription center crease. Grade before defect - VG40. Grade with defect - GD30. *Dick Tracy Comics Monthly #41*, 1951. © Chicago Tribune.

Ink lines in logo letters

Defect: Logo tracing in ink. Grade before defect - VG40. Grade with defect - GD25. *Super Mystery Comics V6#2*, 1946. © Ace Periodicals.

Restapled

Restapled

Loose
staple

Defect: Restapled cover, loose from original staples. Grade before defect - VG50. Grade with defect - GD25. *My Greatest Adventure #51*, 1961. © DC Comics.

Ring
on
cover

Defect: Water ring on cover. Grade before defect - VG40. Grade with defect - GD25. *Eighty Page Giant #3*, 1964. © DC Comics.

Coupon out of back cover

Defect: Coupon cut out of back cover. Grade before defect - VG50. Grade with defect - GD20. *Detective Comics #64*, 1942.

Book-length split spine

Defect: Book-length split spine. Grade before defect - FN55. Grade with defect - GD15. *Master Comics* #11, 1941. © Fawcett Publ.

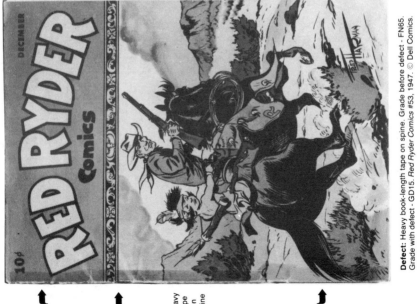

Heavy tape on spine

Defect: Heavy book-length tape on spine. Grade before defect - FN65. Grade with defect - GD15. *Red Ryder Comics* #53, 1947. © Dell Comics.

GRADE: FAIR

Abbreviated Notation: **FR**

Overstreet Numerical Equivalent (**ONE**) range: **14-5**
(**Highest** possible FR grade = 14, **Mid**-grade = 10, **Lowest** possible FR grade = 5)

GRADE DESCRIPTION:
A copy in this grade has all pages and most of the covers, although there may be up to ⅓ of the front cover missing or no back cover, but not both. A comic in this grade may be soiled, ragged, unattractive, creased and/or folded. The centerfold may be missing if it does not affect a story. Spine may be split. Staples may be gone, and/or cover detached. Corners are commonly rounded or absent. Coupons may be cut. Comic books in this condition are often referred to as "reading" or "research copies." Paper quality is often low.

CHECKLIST FOR THE GRADE FAIR:

- ✓ Heavy wear.
- ✓ Basic readability is preserved.
- ✓ Discoloration, fading and/or soiling.
- ✓ Some pieces may be missing.
- ✓ Staples may be degraded or gone.
- ✓ Cover may be detached.
- ✓ Coupon may be cut.
- ✓ The spine may be split.
- ✓ Pages may be brittle around the edges.
- ✓ Tape and other forms of repair are more common than the next higher grade.
- ✓ Fair comics are often faded.
- ✓ Ragged appearance, abrasions and creases.
- ✓ Spine roll common.
- ✓ Centerfold may be missing if it does not interfere with a story.

Note: The demand for comic books in this grade from 1930s through 1960s issues is high.

⊛ *COLLECTOR ALERT:* Comic books described in this grade should be examined for brittleness.

⊛ *COLLECTOR ALERT:* Some Poor condition comics have missing pages unscroupously replaced with pages from a different issue or title to give the appearance of being Fair.

ACCUMULATED DEFECTS RULE:
Books in this grade will not have **all** the listed defects but will have a combination of some of the above defects. The final grade depends on the number and severity of defects listed under the checklist.

GRADE: **FAIR** (ONE - **14**)

Example: Front cover of *Super Comics* #74, 1944. © Dell Publ.
Obvious defects: Loose staples and spine roll. Ragged edges and spine.
Hidden defects: Cover detached from interior pages. First two centerfolds loose.
Centerfold is split through center. A 4'' rip at top of spine through entire book.
OWL: 3.

Rolled spine

Heavy cover wear

Fanned pages

Missing corner piece

Loose staple

Severe staple tear

Long reading creases

Ragged edges

Spine tear

Edge wear, tears & creases

Tear

Corner creases

Exposed loose centerfold

Fanned pages due to rolled spine

Corner crease

Multiple edge tears

Heavy cover wear

Rounded corner

Loose staple

Tear

Many small stress marks along spine, top & bottom of cover

Edge tear

Spine tear

GRADE: **FAIR** (ONE - **14**)

Example: Front cover of *Samson* #12, 1955. © Farrell Publ.
Obvious defects: Chunk missing from cover.
Hidden defects: Cover and centerfold are completely detached.
OWL: 4.

GRADE: **FAIR** (ONE - 13)

Example: Front cover of *Superman's Girl Friend Lois Lane* #63, 1966. © DC Comics.
Obvious defects: Multiple restapling and restaple holes along spine. Extended pages
  on right edge of loose centerfold that was misaligned when restapled.
Hidden defects: None.
OWL: 5.

Shifted
centerfold
restapled
in wrong
location

Restapled
holes

Restapled

Restapled
holes

Restapled

Inked
date
stamp

Ragged
edge

Long
corner
crease

Edge
tears

FAIR (continued) - *Superman's Girl Friend Lois Lane*
Example: Front cover close ups.

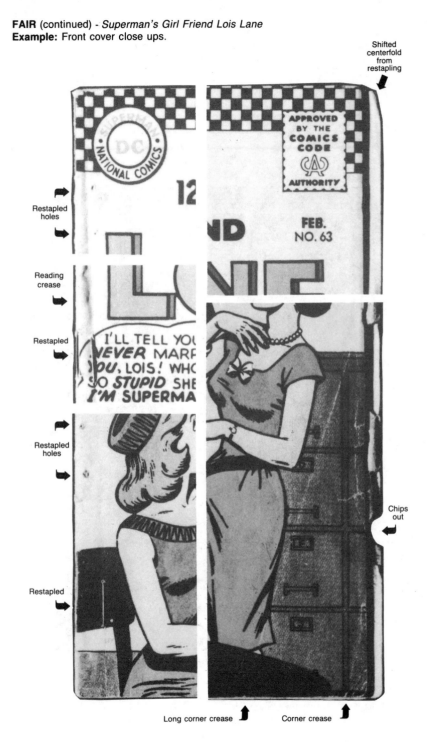

Shifted centerfold from restapling

Restapled holes

Reading crease

Restapled

Restapled holes

Restapled

Chips out

Long corner crease   Corner crease

GRADE: **FAIR** (ONE - 12)

Example: Front cover of *Mystical Tales* #2, 1956. © Marvel Ent. Group.
Obvious defects: Heavy spine abrasion/color scrapes, heavy creasing and cover wear.
Hidden defects: Stains on interior pages. Heavily rusted staples. Multiple interior corner folds. Long rip and hole in front cover.
OWL: 5.

FAIR (continued) - *Mystical Tales*
Example: Back cover.

Book-length crease

Heavily
rusted
staple
& rust
stains

Creases

Corner
creases

Edge tear &
corner crease

Corner
crease

Book-length
crease

Abraded
corner

GRADE: **FAIR** (ONE - **10**)

Example: Front cover of *Prize Comics* #7, 1940. © Prize Publ.
Obvious defects: Ragged spine with multiple tape repairs and piece out of back cover.
Hidden defects: Book length tape inside spine and inside front cover. Rusted staples and centerfold loose. Centerfold is taped at staples.
OWL: 4.

Rounded corner

Pencilled initial

Rounded corner

Tape over staple

Tape on spine

Tape over staple

Long spine split

Edge piece out

Corner piece out

Abraded edge

Corner piece out

Brown, brittle page edge

Tape

Tape bleed through from inside spine

Tape on spine

Tape on spine

Pieces out of edge

Edge tear

Chunk out

GRADE: **FAIR** (ONE - **10**)

Example: Front cover of *Western Hero* #110, 1952. © Fawcett Publ.
Obvious defects: Heavily taped spine with bleed-through.
Hidden defects: Cover taped to inside pages with bleed-through.
OWL: 9.

Inside cover
detail bleed
through

Ragged edge due to
over-cover (See
glossary)

Book-
length
taped
spine

Corner
crease

Corner
crease

Small
corner
piece out

FAIR (continued) - *Western Hero*
Example: Back cover.

Ragged edge due to over-cover
(See glossary)

Abraded
corner

Edge
tears

Book-
length
taped
spine

Edge
tears

Ragged edge due to Marvel chipping

Abraded
corner

GRADE: **FAIR** (ONE - **9**)

Example: Front cover of *Jackie Gleason And The Honeymooners* #1, 1956. © DC Comics.
Obvious defects: Long cover tear and general heavy cover wrinkling and ragged edges.
Hidden defects: Book-length tape on inside spine.
OWL: 4.

GRADE: **FAIR** (ONE - 8)

Example: Front cover of *Detective Comics* #41, 1940. © DC Comics.
Obvious defects: Large chunk out of front cover. Ragged spine.
Hidden defects: None.
OWL: 7.

Edge tears

Split
spine

Loose
staple

Spine
tear

Loose
staple

Color
fleck

Large chunk out

GRADE: FAIR (ONE - 8)

Example: Front cover of *Target Comics* V2#7, 1941. © Novelty Press.
Obvious defects: Heavy water damage on back cover. Ragged spine.
Hidden defects: Book-length taped inside spine split. Wrinkled interior pages.
OWL: 3.

Book is wrinkled due to water damage

FAIR (continued) - *Target Comics*
Example: Back cover.

Heavy book-length water stain   Edge tear   Edge folding   Corner tear

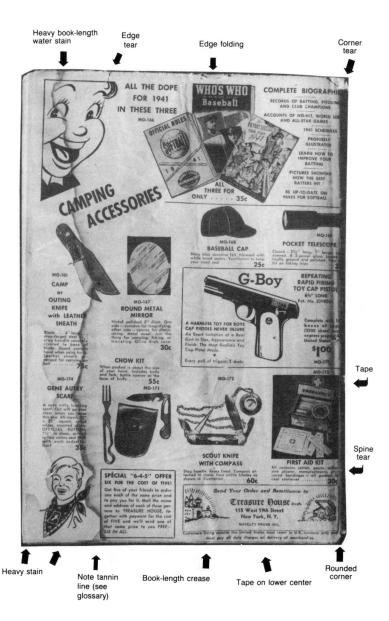

Tape

Spine tear

Heavy stain   Note tannin line (see glossary)   Book-length crease   Tape on lower center   Rounded corner

GRADE: **FAIR** (ONE - 8)

Example: Front cover of *Our Fighting Forces* #12, 1956. © DC Comics.
Obvious defects: Severe pencil marks on covers. Ragged spine.
Hidden defects: Cover is completely detached. Long spine split. First page is heavily soiled. 1'' staple tear through first five pages. Centerfold missing but story not affected.
OWL: 4.

Abraded corner

Ragged edge due to over-cover (See glossary)

Stain spots

Loose staple

Loose staple

2½'' spine split

Piece out

Heavy multiple marks and writing

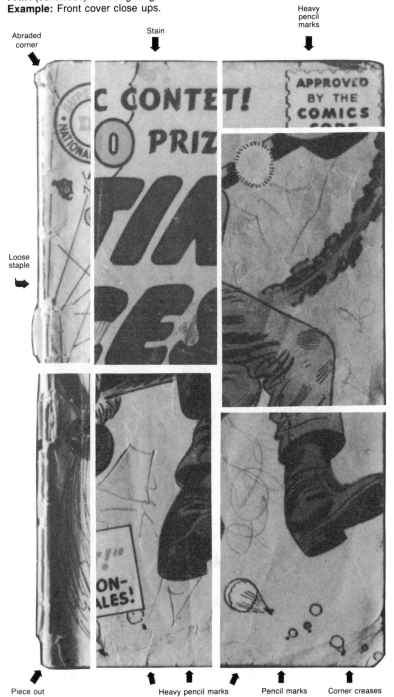

Abraded corner

Stain

Heavy pencil marks

Loose staple

Piece out

Heavy pencil marks

Pencil marks

Corner creases

GRADE: **FAIR** (ONE - 7)

Example: Front cover of *Northwest Mounties* #12, 1954. © St. John Publ.
Obvious defects: Ragged spine and heavy cover wear.
Hidden defects: Cover detached from book. Some inside pages are soiled and loose.
OWL: 5.

GRADE: **FAIR** (ONE - 7)

Example: Front cover of *Superman's Pal, Jimmy Olsen* #87, 1965. © DC Comics.
Obvious defects: Spine is severely split 80% of its length and spine is extremely
  ragged. Three hole punch through entire book near spine.
Hidden defects: Coupon cut from interior page which does not affect story.
OWL: 7.

Hole punched
through book

Pencilled
words

Severe
7½"
spine
split

Folded
edge
tear

1"
tear

Abraded
corner

Hole punched
through book

Multiple
corner
creases

Multiple
corner
creases

GRADE: **FAIR** (ONE - 7)

Example: Front cover of *Eighty Page Giant* #13, 1965. © DC Comics.

Obvious defects: Back cover missing. Ragged spine, spine split and heavy cover abrasion.

Hidden defects: Restapled from upper left corner. Multiple corner folds on interior pages. Chips missing from spine.

OWL: 7.

Spine tear

Heavy abrasion

Corner creases

Square bound

Abraded spine

Book-length reading crease

Abraded corner

Small corner crease   Slight page fanning   Restapled

Back cover   Edge tear
missing

Note: No back cover.

GRADE: **FAIR** (ONE - 5)

Example: Front cover of *Bugs Bunny* #71, 1960. © Warner Bros.
Obvious defects: Large chunk missing from front cover. Cover detached at lower staple.
Hidden defects: Cover loose at lower staple. 4'' split at bottom of spine of first wraparound. Foxing throughout interior pages.
OWL: 4.

Cover creases

Abraded staple holes

Crease

Crease

First wrap-around split

Large chunk out of cover

Corner piece missing

GRADE: FAIR
DEFECT SECTION

The grade of all of the books in this section have (a) dropped from either a higher grade to the Fair grade due to a specific damaging defect, or (b) have dropped a few points within this grade.

Large piece out

Defect: Large chunk out of back cover. Grade before defect - GD25. Grade with defect - FR10. *Gorgo* #2. 1961. © Charlton Comics.

Defect: Long rip and piece out of spine corner. Grade before defect - VG50. Grade with defect - FR14. *War Action #13*, 1953. © Marvel Ent. Group.

Chunk out

Split spine

Long rip

Light center crease

Edge tear

Edge tear

Edge tear

Rolled spine

Chunk out

Rip through entire book

Small piece out

Defect: Chunks out of spine corners. Grade before defect - GD20. Grade with defect - FR12. *Police Comics #71*, 1947. © Quality Comics.

Long diagonal crease

Large coupon cut

Inside paper soiled

Defect: Large coupon missing from back cover. Grade before defect - GD25. Grade with defect - FR9. *Walt Disney's C&S #123*, 1950. © Walt Disney Co.

Logo removed

Defect: Remainders copy ("three-quarter cover"). Grade before defect - FN65. Grade with defect - FR6. *Metal Men #21*, 1966. © DC Comics.

Detect: No back cover. Grade before defect - VG45. Grade with defect - FR5. Marvel Mystery Comics #32, 1942. © Marvel Ent. Group.

Fanned pages caused by rolled spine

Back cover missing

GRADE: POOR
Abbreviated Notation: PR

Overstreet Numerical Equivalent (ONE) range: 4-1
(**Highest** possible PR grade = 4, **Mid**-grade = 3, **Lowest** possible PR grade = 1)

GRADE DESCRIPTION:
Most comic books in this grade have been sufficiently degraded to where there is little or no collector value. Copies in this grade typically have pages and/or part of all of the front cover missing. They may have severe stains, mildew or heavy cover abrasion or having been defaced with paint, varnish, glue, oil, indelible markers or dyes. Other defects often include rips, tears, folding and creasing and even moderate to severe brittleness (where the comic book literally "falls apart" when examined). Comic books in this grade are easily identified by a complete absence of "eye appeal" (see glossary).

CHECKLIST FOR THE GRADE POOR:

- Extreme abrasion and wear.
- Front cover may be gone or coverless.
- Moderate to extreme brittleness.
- Extreme soiling and staining.
- Large chunks missing.
- Extremely ragged spines and edges.
- Extreme fading where the cover becomes almost indiscernible.
- Paint or oil stains.
- Pages may be missing which affect story.
- Cover may be laminated with plastic.
- Heavy water/mildew damage.
- Severe rips, tears, folding and creasing.

Note: Coverless comics are the exception to the "not collectible in Poor" rule. Many collectors want clean, readable, coverless comics that are priced fairly. Coverless copies of key and/or rare comics are in demand by collectors. These enthusiasts also seek coverless comics to retrieve centerfolds, first wrap-arounds, coupons and even staples in order to utilize them in the restoration of other incomplete comics.

COLLECTOR ALERT: When examining comic books for sale, do not remove severely brittle comic books from their protective wrappers. Request that the owner handle the book. There have been reported cases where prospective buyers were held responsible for unavoidable damage to brittle comic books during examination.

GRADE: **POOR** (ONE - 4)

Example: Front cover of *Showcase* #22, 1959. © DC Comics.
Obvious defects: Extreme cover degradation.
Hidden defects: Severe mildew throughout. Coupon cut from back cover. Story
complete and readable.
OWL: 5 (Mildew spots throughout)

Heavy soiling and foxing

Heavy
wrinkling
& loss
of color
due to
water
damage

Heavy soiling and foxing

GRADE: **POOR** (ONE - **3**)

Example: Front cover of *Walt Disney's C&S* #210, 1958. © Walt Disney Co.
Obvious defects: Large chunks out of front cover. Ragged spine and book edges.
Hidden defects: 4'' split spine. Foxing and interior pages torn.
OWL: 5.

Corner
creases

Abraded
cover

Crease

Chunk out
of cover

Spine
roll

Separated
spine

Chunk
out

Severe
staple
tear

Corner
tear

Cover
creases

Cover creases

Corner
wear

GRADE: **POOR** (ONE - 3)

Example: Front cover of *Tales Of The Unexpected* #40, 1959. © DC Comics.
Obvious defects: Spine abrasion and tears.
Hidden defects: First wrap-around missing ruining main feature.
OWL: 5.

Abraded corner

Edge tears

Loose staple

Long spine split

Loose staple

Spine tear

Corner tear

Corner crease

Multiple corner creases

GRADE: **POOR** (ONE - 2)

Example: Front cover of *Ella Cinders* #1, 1948. © St. John.
Obvious defects: Very ragged edges with pieces out. Spine is almost completely
split its entire length.
Hidden defects: Brittle pages.
OWL: 0.

Piece missing

Pieces missing

Chunk out

Spine area soiling

Tear

Piece missing & spine split

Piece missing

Tear

Small pieces missing

Severe edge chipping and paper
color is an indicator of brittleness

Piece missing
and torn spine

Chunk out

Piece
missing

ANC

Multiple
spine
creases

Long
tear

Chunks
out

Split spine
& edge flaking

Piece missing

Pieces missing due
to brittleness

GRADE: **POOR** (ONE - 2)

Example: Front cover of *Red Rabbit Comics* #14, 1950. © J. Charles Laue.
Obvious defects: Ripped spine, almost completely split. Cover completely detached.
Hidden defects: Centerfold missing.
OWL: 4.

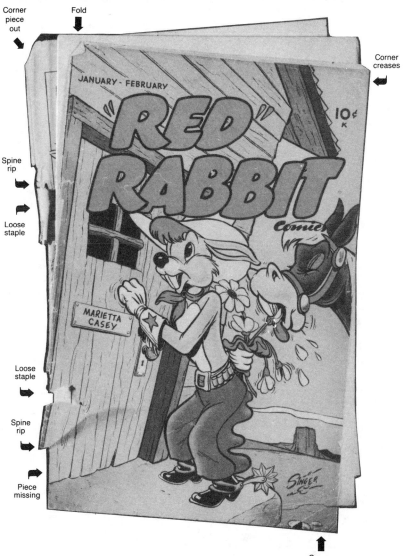

Corner piece out

Fold

Corner creases

Spine rip

Loose staple

Loose staple

Spine rip

Piece missing

Corner creases

Coverless. Coverless comics that are otherwise complete grade PR2 or less. *Cookie*, 1940s. © American Comics Group.

Defect: Bindery defect-severe trimming. Grade before defect - NM94. Grade with defect - PR3. *Walt Disney's D. Duck* #256, 1987. © The Walt Disney Co.

Long spine split & 24 pages missing. Cuts across center of cover. Grade PR1. *Daisy Duck and Uncle Scrooge Showboat* #55, 1961. © Walt Disney Co.

More than ⅓ of cover missing; no back cover and last page missing. Inside pages severely soiled. Grade PR1. *Mickey Mouse* No. 31, 1953. © Walt Disney Co.

GLOSSARY

ABRADED CORNER - Grinding of corner area caused by improper handling or storage.

ABRADED STAPLE HOLE - See "Staple Hole."

ADZINE - A magazine primarily devoted to the advertising of comic books and collectibles as its first publishing priority as opposed to written articles.

ALLENTOWN COLLECTION - A collection discovered in 1987-88 just outside Allentown, Pennsylvania. The Allentown collection consisted of 135 Golden Age comics, characterized by high grade and superior paper quality.

ANILINE - A poisonous oily liquid, colorless when pure, obtained from coal tar and especially from nitro benzene, used in making inks, dyes and perfumes, in certain medicines, in plastics, resins, etc. (See Quinone).

ANNUAL - (1) A book that is published yearly. (2) Some squarebound comics.

ARRIVAL DATE - The date written or stamped on the cover of comics by either the local wholesaler or the retailer. The date precedes the cover date by approximately 15 to 75 days and may vary considerably from one locale to another, or from one year to another.

ASHCAN - A publisher's inhouse facsimile of a proposed new title. Most ashcans have black and white covers stapled to an existing coverless comic on the inside. Other ashcans are totally black and white.

AVERAGE FINE - A term used by some to describe the condition fine minus.

B & W - Abbreviation for "Black and White."

BACK UP FEATURE - A story or character not usually featured on the cover nor as the first story in the comic.

BAXTER PAPER - A high quality, white, heavy paper used in the printing of some comics.

BBC - Abbreviation for "Bottom of Back Cover."

BC - Abbreviation for "Back Cover."

BI-MONTHLY - Published every two months.

BINDER - The person that oversees the bindery process.

BINDER HOLES - Either two or three holes punched into the spine of comics so as to fit them into a two or three ring binder.

BINDER PERFS - See "Perforations."

BINDERY - The location where comic books are assembled, trimmed, and stapled and/or glued.

BINDERY CORNER - Small, triangular spine corner tears that occur during binding.

BINDERY DEFECT - Defects associated with the binding process, including mistrimming, miswrapping, inaccurate stapling, etc.

BINDERY TRIMMING DEFECT TAXONOMY- Comic is not cut/trimmed correctly at the bindery.

Type 1 (cover cut squarely)

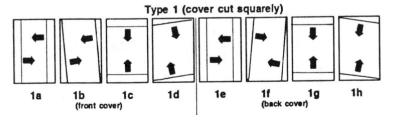

| 1a | 1b | 1c | 1d | 1e | 1f | 1g | 1h |

(front cover)   (back cover)

Type 1 - Cover cut squarely:

    1a. - Cover square—rectangular part of back cover shows along spine or right edge of front cover.

    1b. - Cover square—triangular part of back cover shows along spine or right edge of front cover.

    1c. - Cover square—white unprinted rectangular strip at either top or bottom of front cover indicating that cover travelled before trimming.

    1d. - Cover square—white unprinted triangular strip at either top or bottom of front cover indicating that cover travelled before trimming.

    1e. - Same as 1a but applies to back cover.

1f. - Same as 1b but applies to back cover.
1g. - Same as 1c but applies to back cover.
1h. - Same as 1d but applies to back cover.

Type 2 (cover not cut squarely)

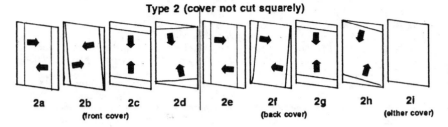

2a	2b	2c	2d	2e	2f	2g	2h	2i
	(front cover)				(back cover)			(either cover)

Type 2 - Cover not cut squarely:
   2a, 2b, 2c, 2d, 2e, 2f, 2g, 2h. - Cover not square/otherwise same as 1a, 1b, 1c, 1d, 1e, 1f, 1g, 1h.
   2i. - Cover not square/no other defects.

BI-WEEKLY - Published every two weeks.

BLACK COVER - Covers with a predominate use of black ink. The black ink has a tendency to show defects more readily than other ink colors. Because of this, high grade comics with black covers are highly prized by collectors.

BLUNTED CORNER - See "Corner Blunting."

BONDAGE COVER - Usually denotes a female in bondage.

BOUND COPY - A copy that has been bound into a book. The process requires that the spine be trimmed off and sometimes sewn into a book-like binding.

BOUND SHORT - See "Siamese Page."

BRITISH ISSUE - Printed for distribution in Great Britain. These copies sometimes have the price in pence instead of cents.

BRITTLENESS - A severe condition of paper deterioration where paper loses its flexibility and thus chips and/or flakes easily.

BRONZE AGE - (1) Non- specific term not in general acceptance by collectors at this writing which denotes comics published from approximately 1970 through 1980. (2) Term which describes the "Age" of comic books after the Silver Age.

BROWNING - (1) The aging of paper characterized by the ever- increasing level of oxidation characterized by darkening. (2) The level of paper deterioration one step more severe than tanning and one step before brittleness.

CAMEO - The brief appearance of one character in the strip of another.

CANADIAN ISSUE - Printed for distribution in Canada. These copies sometimes have no advertising.

CCA - Abbreviation for "The Comics Code Authority."

CENTER CREASE - See "Subscription Crease."

CENTERFOLD - The two folded pages in the center of a comic book at the terminal end of the staples.

CENTER SPREAD - See "Center Fold."

CFO - Abbreviation for "Center Fold Out."

CHIP CUT - Missing piece smaller than 1 square millimeter.

CIRCULATION COPY - Subscription copy.

CIRCULATION FOLD - Subscription fold.

CLASSIC COVER - A cover considered by collectors to be highly desirable because of its subject matter, artwork, historical importance, etc.

CLEANING - A process in which dirt and dust is removed.

COLOR FLAKE - The color layer has been lost, making the white paper substrata visible. Color flakes are larger than one square millimeter and smaller than two square millimeters.

COLOR FLECK - The color layer has been lost, making the white paper substrata visible. Color flecks are no larger than one square millimeter.

COLOR TOUCH - A restoration process by which colored ink is used to hide color flecks, color flakes, and larger areas of missing color. Short for "color touch-up."

COLORIST - Artist that applies color to the black and white pen-and-ink art.

COMIC BOOK DEALER - (1) A seller of comic books. (2) One who makes a living buying and selling comic books.

COMIC BOOK REPAIR - When a tear, loose staple or centerfold has been mended without changing or adding to the original finish of the book. Repair may involve tape, glue or nylon gossamer and is easily detected. It is considered a defect.

COMIC BOOK RESTORATION - Any attempt, whether professional or amateur, to enhance the appearance of a comic book. These procedures may include any or all of the following techniques: Recoloring, adding missing paper, stain, ink, dirt or tape removal, whitening, pressing out wrinkles, staple replacement, trimming, re-glossing, etc. Note: Unprofessional work can lower the value of a book.

COMICS CODE AUTHORITY - The Comics Magazine Association of America. An organization formed in 1954 to review (and possibly censor) comic books before they were printed and distributed. The emblem of the CCA is a white stamp in the upper right hand corner of comics dated after February, 1955. The term "post code" refers to the time after this practice started, or approximately 1955 to the present.

COMPLETE RUN - All issues of a given title.

CON - A convention or public gathering of fans.

CONDITION - The state of preservation of a comic book.

CORNER - See "Abraded Corner."

CORNER BLUNTING - Compression folds at approximately 45 degrees to the ends and sides of the comic, as if the corner of the comic were dropped against a hard surface.

CORNER CREASE - Permanent crease located within 1" of a corner. Usually the upper right hand corner or the lower right hand corner.

CORNER FOLD - A linear dent indicating folding within 1" of the corner. Usually the upper right hand corner or the lower right hand corner.

COSMIC AEROPLANE COLLECTION - A collection from Salt Lake City, Utah characterized by the moderate to high grade copies with pencil check marks in the margins of inside pages. It is thought that these comics were kept by a commercial illustration school and the check marks were placed beside panels that instructors wanted students to draw.

COSTUMED HERO - A costumed crime fighter with "developed" human powers instead of "super" powers.

COUPON CUT - Coupon has been neatly removed with scissors or razor blade (from anywhere in the comic) as opposed to having been ripped out.

COUPON MISSING - See "Coupon Cut."

COVER GLOSS - The reflective quality of the cover ink.

COVER LOOSE - (1) Cover has become completely detached from the staples. (2) Cover moves around on the staples but is not completely detached from the staples.

COVER MISSING - See "No Cover."

COVER OFF - Cover is completely detached from the staples.

COVER REATTACHED - Cover has been repaired/restored to hold staples and reattached to comic interior.

COVER TRIMMED - Cover has been reduced in size by neatly cutting away rough or damaged edges.

CREASE - A fold which causes ink removal usually resulting in a white line. See "Corner Crease" and "Reading Crease."

CROSSOVER - A story where one character appears prominently in the story of another character (also called "x-over").

CVR - Abbreviation for "cover."

DATE STAMP - Arrival or other date printed in ink somewhere in or on the comic by use of a stamp and stamp pad.

DEALER - See "Comic Book Dealer."

DEACIDIFICATION - Several different processes that reduce acidity in paper.

DEBUT - The first time that a character appears anywhere.

DEFECT - Any fault or flaw that detracts from perfection.

DEFECTIVES - Comics which, through flaws, are imperfect.

DEFORMED STAPLE - Staple that has not penetrated all the pages properly or is bent and/or misshapen. See "Shallow Staple."

DENT - An indentation, usually on the cover, that does not penetrate the paper nor remove any material or gloss.

DENVER COLLECTION - A collection consisting primarily of early high grade number one issues bought at auction in Pennsylvania by a Denver, Colorado dealer.

DIMPLE - A surface indentation on the cover. Usually caused by excessive thumb/finger pressure at the edge of the cover.

DIRTY - Inorganic and organic substances that can be removed from paper by cleaning.

DISTRIBUTOR PAINTED STRIPES - See "Distributor Stripes."

DISTRIBUTOR STRIPES - Color brushed or sprayed on the edges of comic book stacks by the distributor/wholesaler to code them for expedient exchange at the sales racks. Typical colors are red, orange, yellow, green, blue, and purple. Distributor Stripes are not a defect.

DOUBLE - A duplicate copy of the same comic book.

DOUBLE COVER - Bindery "defect" where two covers are stapled to the comic interior instead of the usual one. Exterior cover often protects interior cover from wear and damage. Considered a desirable situation by some collectors and may increase collector value. Also see "Multiple covers."

DRUG PROPAGANDA STORY - A comic makes an editorial stand about drug use.

DRUG USE STORY - Shows the actual use of drugs: shooting, taking a trip, harmful effects, etc.

DRY PRESS - Machine used to flatten out comics with rolled spine and folds.

DUOTONE - Printed with black and one other color of ink. This process was common in comics printed in the 1930s.

DUST SHADOW - Darker, usually linear area at the edge of some comics stored in stacks. Some portion of the cover was not covered by the comic immediately above it and was exposed to settling dust particles. Also see "Oxidation Shadow" and "Sun Shadow."

EDGAR CHURCH COLLECTION - See "Mile High Collection."

ERASER MARK - Damage left when pencil marks are removed from the cover or inside of a comic. Most identifiable when cover gloss is dulled.

EXTENDERS - See "Staple Extenders."

EYE APPEAL - A term which refers to the overall look of a comic book when held at approximately arms length. A comic may have nice eye appeal, yet have hidden defects which reduce grade.

FADED COVER - See "Fading."

FADING - Color fading due to exposure to sunlight or certain fluorescent lights which give off a moderate to high percentage of ultra violet light.

FANNED PAGES - A condition caused by a rolled spine which progressively pulls interior pages away from the edge creating a "fanned" appearance.

FANZINE - An amateur fan publication.

FC - Abbreviation for "Front Cover."

FILE COPY - A high grade comic originating from the publisher's file. Not all file copies are in pristine mint condition. Note: An arrival date on the cover of a comic does not indicate that it is a file copy.

FINGER OILS - Body oils left when handling comics with bare hands. Oil accelerates the collection of dust and dirt.

FIRST APPEARANCE - See "Debut."

FLASHBACK - When a previous story is recalled.

FLECK - See "Color Fleck."

FOLDING ERROR - A bindery defect in which the comic is folded off- center, resulting in part of the front cover appearing on the back cover, or more seriously, part of the back cover appearing on the front cover.

FOLDED OFF-CENTER - See "Folding Error."

FOLDS - Linear dents in paper that does not result in the loss of ink. Not a crease.

FOLIO - A sheet of paper, folded once in the middle, making 2 leaves or 4 pages. 32 interior pages are made up of 8 folios. The centerfold, cover, and first wraparound are examples of folios.

FOUR COLOR - Series of comics produced by Dell characterized by hundreds of different features. Named after the four color process of printing. See "One Shots."

FOUR COLOR PROCESS - Name given to the process of printing with the three primary colors (red, yellow, and blue) plus black.

FOXING - Defect caused by mold growth which results in a spotting effect usually at the edges of comic books.

FREEZE DRY - Process used to preserve paper that has been wet before mildew damage can occur.

FUMETTI - Illustration system in which individual frames of a film are colored and used for individual panels to make a comic book story. The most famous example is DC's Movie Comics 1-6 from 1939.

G.A. - Golden Age.

GENRE - Categories of comic book subject matter; e.g. Science Fiction, Super Hero, Romance, Funny Animal, Teenage Humor, Crime, War, Western, Mystery, Horror, etc.

GIVEAWAY - Type of comic book intended to be given away as a premium or promotional device instead of being sold.

GLASSES ATTACHED - In 3D comics, the special blue and red cellophane glasses are still attached to the comic. More desirable than ''Glasses Detached.''

GLASSES DETACHED - In 3D comics, the special blue and red cellophane glasses are not still attached to the comic. Less desirable than ''Glasses Attached.''

GLUE or GLUED - Restoration method in which some form of glue was used to repair or reinforce a comic book defect.

GOLDEN AGE - Although open to interpretation, most collectors and comic book historians define it as the period of comic book publishing from June, 1938 (Action #1) until the end of WWII or approximately the end of 1945.

GREASE PENCIL - A wax based marker commonly used to write on cardboard.

GREASE PENCIL ON COVER - Indicates that someone marked the cover of a comic with a grease pencil, usually with a resale price or an arrival date.

GREY TONE COVER - A cover art style in which pencil or charcoal underlies the normal line drawing. Used to enhance the effects of light and shadow, thus producing a ''richer'' quality. These covers, prized by most collectors, are sometimes referred to as ''painted covers'' but are not actually painted. See ''Painted Covers.''

HEADLIGHTS - Protruding breasts.

HEAVY CREASING - A crease that is longer than 2 inches.

HRN - Abbreviation for highest reorder number. Most often used to distinguish first editions from later printings in Gilberton's Classic Comics series.

IBC - Abbreviation for ''Inside Back Cover.''

IFC - Abbreviation for ''Inside Front Cover.''

ILLO - Abbreviation for ''Illustration.''

INDICIA - Publishing and title information usually located at the bottom of the first page or the bottom of the inside front cover. In rare cases and some pre-1938 comics, it was sometimes located on internal pages.

INFINITY COVER - Shows a scene that repeats itself to infinity.

INITIALS ON COVER - Someone's initials in pencil, pen, or grease pencil on the cover.

INIT. ON CVR - Short for ''Initials on Cover.''

INK SKIP - Printing defect in which the printing roller momentarily receives no ink causing a streak or blank spot.

INK SMUDGE - Printing defect in which ink is smeared, usually by handling before the ink is completely dry. These commonly look like fingerprints.

INKER - Artist that does the inking.

INTRO - See ''Debut.''

INVESTMENT GRADE COPY - (1) Comic of sufficiently high grade and demand to be viewed by collectors as instantly liquid should the need arise to sell. (2) In very fine or better condition. (3) Comic purchased primarily to achieve a profit.

ISSUE NUMBER - The actual edition number of a given title.

ISH - Short for ''Issue.''

JLA - Justice League of America.

JLI - Justice League International.

JOINED PAGES - (1) Bindery defect in which pages are ''trimmed long'' and are not separated at right hand corner(s) or along right edge. See ''Siamese Pages''. (2) A rare printing defect where a new roll of paper is glued to the spent roll while still on the press. This glued intersection appears as a vertical ''stripe'' of double thick newsprint on one of the interior pages.

JSA - Justice Society of America.

KEY - See ''Key Issue.''

KEY BOOK - See ''Key Issue.''

KEY ISSUE - An issue that contains a first appearance, origin, or other historically or artistically important feature considered especially desirable by collectors.

LAMINATED - Clear plastic with adhesive used by early collectors to protect comics. An outdated and destructive technique which virtually eliminates collector value.

LARSON COPY - Pedigreed copy with the initials or name of its original owner, Lamont Larson.

LATERAL BAR - See "Staple Lateral Bar."

LBC - Abbreviation for "Lower or Left Side or Edge Of Back Cover."

LETTER COL - See "Letter Column."

LETTER COLUMN - A feature in a comic book that prints and sometimes responds to letters written by its readers.

LFC - Abbreviation for "Lower or Left Side or Edge Of Front Cover."

LFT - Abbreviation for "Left."

LIGHT CREASING - A crease 2" long or less.

LINE DRAWN COVER - A cover published in the traditional way where pencil sketches are overdrawn with india ink and then colored. See also "Grey Tone Cover," "Photo Cover," and "Painted Cover."

LLBC - Abbreviation for "Lower Left Corner of Back Cover."

LOGO - The title of a strip or comic book as it appears on the cover or title page.

LOGO CUT - See "Remainders."

LOOSE STAPLES - Staples that can be easily moved and no longer hold comic pages tightly. See also "popped staple."

LRBC - Abbreviation for "Lower Right Corner Of Back Cover."

LRFC - Abbreviation for "Lower Right Corner Of Front Cover."

LSH - Legion of Super-Heroes.

MAGIC LIGHTNING COLLECTION - A collection of high grade 1950s comics from the San Francisco area.

MANUFACTURING FOLD - A defect in which some page(s) of the comic (usually the cover) is folded during the printing and/or the paper manufacturing process.

MARVEL CHIPPING - A bindery (trimming/cutting) defect that causes a series of chips and tears at the top, bottom, and right edge of the cover. This is caused where the cutting blade of an industrial paper trimmer becomes dull. Dubbed "Marvel chipping" because it can occur quite often with that companys comics from the late 50s and early 60s but can also occur with any companys comic books from the late 1940s through the middle 1960s.

MAVERICK PAGES - Interior pages that are not the same size or shape as the majority of the rest of the pages. Most commonly a bindery defect.

MAVERICK SIGNATURE - See "Maverick Pages."

MAVERICK STAPLE - See "Deformed Staple."

MID SPINE - Between the staples.

MILE HIGH COLLECTION - Collection discovered in Denver, Colorado in 1977, originally owned by Mr. Edgar Church. Comics from this collection are now famous for extremely white pages, fresh smell, and beautiful cover ink reflectivity.

MISCUT - Bindery defect where cover and/or pages are not cut square or are cut to wrong size.

MISTRIMMED - See "Miscut."

MISWRAPPED - Bindery defect where staple and fold do not intersect the center of the cover causing some of the back cover to appear on the front of the comic or some of the front cover to "ride around" to the back.

MOISTURE DAMAGE -Wrinkling and/or stains caused by absorption of a liquid.

MOISTURE RING - Circular wrinkling and/or stain caused by absorption of moisture usually from the bottom of a cup or glass.

MOTH BALL SMELL - The odor imparted to some comic books because of their storage with moth balls. Some comics from specific collections can be identified by this characteristic odor.

MULTIPLE BINDERY STAPLES - Bindery defect in which the comic book is stapled additional times unnecessarily.

MULTIPLE READING CREASES - See "Reading Creases."

MYLARTM- An inert, very hard, space age plastic used to make high quality protective bags and sleeves used for comic book storage. MylarTM is a trademark of the Dupont Co.

MYLAR SLEEVE - See "Mylar™."

NAME STAMP - Indicates that an ink stamp with someone's name (and sometimes address) has been stamped in or on the comic book.

NC - Abbreviation for "No cover." See "Cover Missing."

ND - See "No Date."

NIT-PICKER - Collector/Investor who is never satisfied with the condition of a comic book, regardless of quality.

NN - See "No Number."

NO COVER -Cover missing.

NO DATE - When there is no date given on the cover or indicia page.

NO NUMBER - When there is no number given on the cover or indicia page. These are usually first issues or one-shots.

OFF-CENTER FOLDING - See "Folding Error."

OFF REGISTER - See "Out Of Register."

OFF-SET COVER - See "Off-Set Folding."

OIL DAMAGE - See "Oil Stain."

OIL STAIN - A defect in which oil has penetrated the cover and /or interior pages, causing them to become translucent in the area of the stain.

ONE - Overstreet Numerical Equivalency.

ONE SHOT - When only one issue is published of a title, or when a series is published where each issue is a different title (e.g. Dell Four Color Comics).

ORIGIN - When the story of a character's creation is given.

OVER-COVER - Condition common in 1950s comic books where the cover extends approximately one sixteenth of an inch beyond the interior pages. Because this margin is unsupported by the interior pages it is more susceptible to damage.

OVER GUIDE - When a comic book is priced at a value over guide list.

OVERSTREET - Slang for The Comic Book Price Guide.

OWL - Overstreet Whiteness Level.

OXIDATION SHADOW - Darker, usually linear area at the edge of some comics stored in stacks. Some portion of the cover was not covered by the comic immediately above it and was exposed to the air. Also see "Dust Shadow" and "Sun Shadow."

PAGES MISSING - One or more pages have been removed from a comic.

PAGES OUT OF ORDER - A rare bindery defect in which the pages of a comic book are bound together in the wrong order. See "POOO."

PAGES TRIMMED - The top, bottom and right-hand edge of the comic (or possibly interior pages) have been trimmed with a paper cutter, hand blade, or pneumatic cutter to hide edge defects.

PAGES UPSIDE DOWN - A rare bindery defect in which the cover orientation is reversed relative to the orientation of the interior pages.

PAINTED COVER - (1) Cover taken from an actual painting instead of a line drawing. (2) Inaccurate name for a grey toned cover.

PANELOLIGIST - One who researches comic books and/or comic strips.

PANNAPICTAGRAPHIST - One who collects comic books.

PAPER ABRASION - Rough patch or area where the paper has been abraded on a rough surface leaving a rough texture that is often faded.

PAPER COVER - Comic book cover made from the same newsprint as interior pages. These books are extremely rare in high grade.

PARADE OF PLEASURE - A book about the censorship of comics.

PEDIGREE - Status given to certain highly publicized and usually high grade comic book collections/finds.

PEDIGREED COMIC - A comic coming from a pedigreed collection.

PEDIGREED COPY - See "Pedigreed Comic."

PENCILLER - Artist that does the pencils.

PERFECT BINDING - Pages are glued to the cover as opposed to being stapled to the cover. Also called "square bound" and "square back" comics.

PERFORATIONS - Small hole at the page margins which sometimes occur as part of the manufacturing process. Not considered a defect. Perforations are sometimes used to tell if a comic is an unread copy. In such a copy tell-tale clicks are heard when the book is opened for the first time as the perforations separate.

PG - Abbreviation for "page."

PHOTO COVER - Made from a photograph instead of a line drawing or painting.

PHOTO REACTIVE COLORS - See "Photo Reactive Inks."

PHOTO REACTIVE INKS - Certain inks used in the printing of comics that contain a higher proportion of metals thus decreasing their stability and resistance to fading. Comics with these inks/colors commonly have faded covers. Examples are: "DC dark green" (e.g. Showcase #8, Superman #100), blue (Showcase #13), purple (Showcase #14), and orange-red (Showcase #4).

PICKLE SMELL - A colloquial description of the odor of ascetic acid, often associated with browning and/or brittle paper.

PICTORIAL COVER - Another term for photo cover. See "Photo Cover."

PNEUMATIC CUTTER - An industrial tool used to shear large amounts of paper.

POC - Abbreviation for "pencil on cover."

POLYPROPALENE - A type of plastic used in the manufacture of comic book bags. Now considered harmful to paper and not recommended for long term storage of comics.

POOO - Abbreviation for "Pages Out Of Order," a rare bindery defect in which the cover from one comic is stapled to the interior pages of another comic.

POP - Abbreviation for the "anti-comic book" book *PARADE OF PLEASURE*.

POPPED STAPLE - A term used to describe a condition where the cover has split at the staple and has become detached or "popped loose."

POST CODE - Describes comics published after February 1955 and usually displaying the CCA "stamp" in the upper right-hand corner.

POST GOLDEN AGE - Comic books published between 1945 and 1950.

POST SILVER AGE - Comic books published after 1969.

POUGHKEEPSIE - Refers to a large collection of Dell Comics' "file copies" believed to have originated from the warehouse of Western Publishing in Poughkeepsie, NY.

PRE-CODE - Describes comics published before March 1955.

PRE-GOLDEN AGE - Comic books published prior to Action #1 (June, 1938).

PRE-HERO - A term coined by collectors and in general use by 1983 to describe More Fun 1-51 (pre-Spectre), Adventure 1-39 (pre-Sandman), and Detective 1-26 (pre-Batman). It was later applied (1984-85) to Strange Tales 1-100 (pre-Human Torch). Journey Into Mystery 1-82 (pre-Thor), Tales To Astonish #1-35 (pre-Ant Man), and Tales of Suspense #1-38 (pre-Iron Man). The term is actually inaccurate because technically there were "heroes" in the above books.

PRE-HERO MARVEL - A term used to describe Strange Tales 1-100 (pre-Human Torch), Journey Into Mystery 1-82 (pre-Thor) Tales To Astonish 1-35 (pre-Ant Man), and Tales Of Suspense 1-38 (pre-Iron Man).

PRE-SILVER AGE - Comic books published between 1950 and Showcase #4 (1956).

PRICE STICKERS - Adhesive backed stickers applied to comic covers to alter the cover price. Some collectors view them as a defect.

PRINTERS SMUDGE - See "Ink Smudge."

PRINTING DEFECT - A defect caused by the printing process. Examples would include paper wrinkling, mis-cut edges, mis-folded spine, untrimmed pages, off-registered color, off-centered trimming, mis-folded and mis-bound pages. It should be noted that these are defects that lower the grade of the book.

PRINT THROUGH - The printing on the inside of the front cover is visible (to varying degrees) from the front cover as if one were "looking through" the front cover. Not always considered a defect. See "Transparent Cover."

PROGRESSIVE ROLLED SPINE - Spine roll is more pronounced on one end than the other.

PROVENANCE - When the owner of a book is known and is stated for the purpose of authenticating and documenting the history of the book. Example: A book from the Stan Lee or Forrest Ackerman collection would be an example of a value-adding provenance.

PULP - Cheaply produced magazine made from low grade newsprint. The term comes from the wood pulp that was used in the paper manufacturing process.

PUZZLE FILLED IN - Game or puzzle that has been written on, thus reducing the value of the comic.

QUARTERLY - Published every three months (four times a year).

QUINONE - The substance in ink that promotes oxidation and discoloration and is associated with transfer stains. (2) A yellowish, crystalline compound with an irritating odor, obtained by the oxidation of aniline, and regarded as a benzene with two hydrogen atoms replaced by two oxygen atoms. It is used in tanning and making dyes. Quinone will oxidize another material and be itself reduced to hydroquinone. (See Aniline).

R - See "Reprint."

RARE - Very few copies in existence.

RAT CHEW - Damage caused by the gnawing of rats and mice.

RBC - Abbreviation for "Right Side or Edge of Back Cover."

RBCC - Abbreviation for "Rockets Blast Comic Collector," one of the first and the most prominent adzine instrumental in developing the early comic book market.

READING COPY - A comic that is in Fair to Good condition (**ONE** 5-34) and is often used for research. The condition has been sufficiently reduced to the point where general handling will not degrade it further.

READING CREASES - Book-length, vertical front cover creases at staples, caused by bending cover over staples. Square-bounds receive these creases by just opening the cover too far to the left.

RECESSED STAPLES - When staple lateral bar penetrates below the plane of the cover without breaking through.

REGLOSSING - A repair technique where silicone or other clear sprays are applied to comic book covers in an attempt to restore cover ink reflectivity. Generally not viewed as an ethical practice and reduces value.

REMAINDERS - Comic books that "remain" unsold at the newsstand. In the past the top 1/4 to 1/3 of the cover (or in some cases the entire cover) was removed and returned to the publisher for credit. This practice is the reason many comics from 1936-1965 are sometimes found as coverless copies or 3/4 cover copies.

REMAINDERS COPY - See "Remainders."

REPRINT COMICS - Comic books that contain newspaper strip reprints.

RESEARCH COPY - See "Reading Copy."

RESTORATION - The fine art of repairing a comic to look as close as possible to its original condition.

RESTORED COPY - A comic book that has had restoration work.

RETURN COPY - See "Remainders."

RETURN - See "Remainders."

REVIVAL - An issue that begins republishing a comic book character after a period of dormancy.

RFC - Abbreviation for "Right Side or Edge of Front Cover."

RICE PAPER - A thin, transparent paper commonly used by restorers to repair tears and replace small pieces on covers and pages of comic books.

RIP - Uneven rough tear. Different from a split or cut.

ROLLED SPINE - A condition where the left edge of a comic book curves toward the front or back. A defect caused by folding back each page as the comic was read. See "Progressive Rolled Spine."

ROUGH SPINE - See "Abraded Spine."

ROUND BOUND - Standard saddle stitch binding typical of most comics. (See also "Square Bound").

ROUNDED CORNER - See "Abraded Corner."

RT - Abbreviation for "right."

RUN - A group of comics of one title where most or all of the title are present. (See "Complete Run").

RUST MIGRATION - Rust stains have moved from the staples to the paper.

RUST STAIN - (1) Red-brown stain caused by proximity to a rusty object. (2) Stain associated with rusty staples. A defect.

RUSTY STAPLES - Staples that have oxidized through exposure to moisture in the air.

S.A. - See "Silver Age."

SADDLE STITCH - The staple binding of magazines and comic books.

SCARCE - Not enough copies available to meet demand.

SCI FI - Short for "Science Fiction."

SCRAPED STAPLE - Staple which has had rust or other discoloration removed by scraping the surface. This condition is readily identifiable under a hand lens.

SCUFF - Or "paper scuff." Light paper abrasion.

SEDUCTION OF THE INNOCENT - Book about the censorship of comics published in 1953.

SET - (1) Complete run of a given title. (2) A grouping of comics for sale.

SEWN SPINE - A comic with many spine perforations where binders thread held it into a bound volume. A defect.

SF - Abbreviation for "Science Fiction."

SHALLOW STAPLE - Staple that has not penetrated all of the pages and is not visible at the centerfold. (See "Deformed Staple").

SIAMESE PAGES - Bindery defect in which pages are "trimmed long" and are not separated at right hand corner(s) or along right edge. (See "Joined Pages").

SIG - Short for "signature."

SIGNATURE DUPLICATED - A rare bindery defect in which a group of pages (signature) is inadvertently duplicated. This may also displace and/or replace an adjacent signature. (See "Signatures").

SIGNATURE OUT OF ORDER - A rare bindery defect in which signatures of pages are bound in the wrong sequence. For example, a 32 page comic book with this defect usually has pages in the following order: 9-16, 1-8, 25-32, 17-24.

SIGNATURE REVERSED - A rare bindery defect in which the orientation of one of the signatures is reversed and appears upside down and backwards. (See "Signatures").

SIGS - See "Signatures."

SIGNATURES - A large sheet of paper printed with four or a multiple of four pages. When folded it becomes a section of one comic book.

SILVER AGE - (1) The period of time in comic book history (late 1950s and early 1960s) characterized by the re-birth of 1940s comic book heroes. (2) Sept-Oct 1956 (Showcase #4) through 1969. (3) 1955 through 1969.

SIZING - The glaze applied to newsprint at the end of the manufacturing process.

SLICK COVER - Any cover that is made from clay coated paper stock.

SMOKE DAMAGE - Grey or black discoloration caused by smoke. A defect.

SOILING - Organic and inorganic substances and residues on the surface of the paper. Different than stains, smudges, and mildew.

SOTI - Abbreviation for the book *SEDUCTION OF THE INNOCENT*.

SPINE - The left-hand edge of the comic that will not open.

SPINE CHIP - A small piece missing from the area of the spine.

SPINE ROLL - See "Rolled Spine" and "Progressive Rolled Spine."

SPINE SPLIT - Even separation at the spine fold, commonly above or below the staple.

SPINE STRESS - A small fold, usually less than 1/4 inch long perpendicular to the spine.

SPLASH - See "Splash Panel."

SPLASH PAGE - A splash panel that takes up the entire page. See "Splash Panel."

SPLASH PANEL - (1) The first panel of a comic book story, usually larger than other panels and usually containing the title of the story. The splash panel may also contain artist and writer credits and the name of the feature. (2) An oversized interior panel.

SPLIT SPINE - See "Spine Split."

SQUARE BACK - See "Perfect Binding."

SQUARE BOUND - See "Perfect Binding."

STAINS - Discoloration caused by a foreign substance.

STAMP PAGE - Page devoted to the sale and discussion of stamp collecting. Common in comics of the 1930s.

STAPLE - See "Deformed Staple" and "Recessed Staple."

STAPLE EXTENDERS - The portion of the staple that actually penetrates the paper and can be seen at the centerfold. The portion of the staple that is bent either upwards or downwards toward the center of the staple.

STAPLE HOLE - A punched out area in cover and interior pages caused by staple extender. This hole becomes enlarged (abraded) when staples are removed and replaced several times.

STAPLE LATERAL BAR - The portion of the staple that does not penetrate the paper and lies on top of the cover parallel to the spine. The part of the staple visible on the outside of the comic.

STAPLE PAGE - Term used by early collectors to describe the centerfold.

STAPLE REINFORCED - (1) To strengthen with additional materials the cover paper at the site of staple contact. (2) To strengthen with additional materials the centerfold and/or other pages at the points of staple contact.

STAPLE RUST MIGRATION - Rust stains have moved from the staple to the paper.

STAPLE TEAR - Most often indicates paper separation at the staple.

STAPLE POPPED - Staple tear. Staple has "popped" loose from the cover.

STICKER ON COVER - Price or other sticker adhered to cover.

STORE STAMP - Store name (and sometimes address and telephone number) stamped in ink via rubber stamp and stamp pad.

STRESS LINES - Light, tiny wrinkles occuring along the spine, projecting from the staples or appearing anywhere on the covers of a comic book.

STRESS SPLIT - Any clean paper separation caused by pressure. Most common at the spine.

SUBSCRIPTION CENTER CREASE - See "Subscription Copy."

SUBSCRIPTION COPY - A comic sent through the mail direct from the publisher or publisher's agent. Most are folded in half causing a subscription crease or fold running down the center of the comic from top to bottom.

SUBSCRIPTION FOLD - See "Subscription Copy." Differs from "Subscription Crease" in that no ink is missing as a result of the folding.

SUN SHADOW - Darker, usually linear area at the edge of some comics stored in stacks. Some portion of the cover was not covered by the comic immediately above it and was exposed to the sun. (Also see "Dust Shadow" and "Oxidation Shadow").

SUPER-HERO - A costumed crime fighter with powers beyond those of mortal man.

SUPER-VILLAIN - A costumed criminal with powers beyond those of mortal man. The antithesis of Super-Hero.

SUPPLE - The condition of paper with little or no deterioration. Bendable, pliant, and limber. The opposite of "Brittle."

SWIPE - a panel, sequence, or story obviously borrowed from previously published material.

TANNIN LINE - A brownish stain line of tannin that occurs when wet comic book paper drys.

TAPE RESIDUE - Adhesive substance from cellophane tape which has penetrated paper fibers.

TAPE STAIN - See "Tape Residue."

TOBC - Abbreviation for "Top of Back Cover."

TEAR - an irregular separation of the paper. Different from a split or cut.

TEAR AT STAPLE - See "Staple Tear."

TEAR SEALED - A tear that has been glued together.

TEXT ILLO - A drawing or small panel in a text story that almost never has a dialogue balloon.

TEXT PAGE - A page with no panels or drawings.

TEXT STORY - A story with few if any illustrations commonly used as filler material during the first three decades of comics.

TOFC - Abbreviation for "Top of Front Cover."

3-D COMIC - Comic art that is drawn and printed in two-color layers, producing a true 3-D effect when viewed through special glasses.

3-D EFFECT COMIC - Comic art that is drawn to appear in 3-D, but isn't.

THREE FOURTHS COVER - See "Remainders."

TITLE - The name of the comic book.

TITLE PAGE - First page of a story showing the title of the story.

TOS - (1) Abbreviation for "tape on spine." (2) Abbreviation for "Tales of Suspense."

TRANSFER STAIN - Ink from the first page rubs off onto the inside front cover causing certain portions to appear yellowed. Often mistaken for deterioration. Can also occur on inside back cover.

TRANSPARENT COVER - The printing on the inside front cover is visible (to varying degrees) from the front cover. Not always considered a defect. See "Print Through."

TRIMMED - (1) A bindery process which separates top, right, and bottom of pages and cuts comic books to the proper size. (2) A repair process in which defects along the edges of a comic book are removed with the use of scissors, razor blades, and/or paper cutters. Comic books which have been repaired in this fashion are considered defectives.

TTA - Abbreviation for "Tales to Astonish."

TWO THIRDS COVER - See "Remainders."

ULBC - Abbreviation for "Upper Left Corner of Back Cover."

ULFC - Abbreviation for "Upper Left Corner of Front Cover."

UNDER GUIDE - When a comic book is priced at a value less than guide list.

UPGRADE - To obtain another copy of the same comic book in a higher grade.

URBC - Abbreviation for "Upper Right Corner of Back Cover."

URFC - Abbreviation for "Upper Right Corner of Front Cover."

VINEGAR SMELL - The smell of acetic acid in newsprint that is deteriorating.

WANT LIST - A listing of comics needed by a collector. A list of comics that a collector is interested in purchasing.

WAREHOUSE COPY - Originating from a publisher's warehouse; similar to file copy.

WATER DAMAGE - See "Moisture Damage."

WHITE COVER - Describes certain comics where white is the predominant color. These covers are easily stained and/or damaged and readily show wear. Because they rarely occur in high grade, white covers are in great demand by collectors.

WHITE MOUNTAIN COLLECTION - A collection of 1950s and 1960s comics which originated in New England.

WHITE PAGES - A term used to describe interior pages in the best state of preservation. The preferred state of interior pages.

WHITENESS - See "Whiteness Level."

WHITENESS LEVEL - The whiteness of interior pages compared against a whiteness standard.

WORM HOLE - Small holes eaten into paper caused by a variety of insects and boring worms. Most worm hole damage is actually caused by termites.

WRONG COVER - A rare bindery defect in which the cover from one comic is stapled to the interior pages of another comic.

X-OVER - Short for "crossover."

ZINE - Short for "Fanzine."

CROSS INDEX OF COMIC BOOK COVERS

Title	Page #	Title	Page #
Ace Comics #5	140	Batman #153	116
Ace Comics #75	129	Blue Ribbon #1	73
Ace Comics #118	202	Boy Love's Girl #27	207
Ace Comics #121	126	The Brave And The Bold #28	152
Action Comics #4	191	Bugs Bunny #71	278
Action Comics #47	176	Captain America #100	66
Adventure Comics #33	249	Challengers Of The Unknown #4	171
Adventure Comics #79	134	Comic Cavalcade #11	98
Adventure Comics #218	243	Comic Cavalcade #13	163
Adventures Into Weird Worlds #6	83	Comic Cavalcade #21	198
Adventures Of Superman #475	209	The Comics #5	121
All-American Comics #28	128	Comics Magazine #2	100
All Good Comics nn, 1944	75	Cookie, 1940s	290
All Select #2	43	Dale Evans #1	193
All Star Comics #24	205	Daring Mystery Comics #8	200
All Winners #6	165	Dell Giant #55	290
Amazing Mystery Funnies #1	189	Detective Comics #4	181
Amazing Mystery Funnies #3	214	Detective Comics #22	143
The Amazing Spider-Man #5	55	Detective Comics #24	102
The Amazing Spider-Man Annual #2	85	Detective Comics #31	110
America's Greatest Comics #3	194	Detective Comics #41	269
Apache Kid #13	167	Detective Comics #46	201
Archie's Christmas Stocking #1	149	Detective Comics #64	253
The Atom #7	55	Detective Comics #225	183
Atomic Comics #4	159	Detective Comics #316	180
The Avengers #11	41	Dick Tracy Comics Monthly #41	251
Batman #36	162	Doll Man Quarterly #2	234
Batman #73	160	Doll Man Quarterly #12	215
Batman #152	123	Donald Duck #256	290

CROSS INDEX OF COMIC BOOK COVERS (continued)

Title	Page #	Title	Page #
Down With Crime #1	166	Rip Hunter...Time Master #1	147
Dynamo #2	64	Rocket Ship X #1	199
Eighty Page Giant #3	252	Roly Poly Comics #10	122
Eighty Page Giant #13	276	Samson #12	258
Ella Cinders #1	287	Sensation Comics #35	205
Famous Funnies #22	250	Sensation Comics #62	212
Famous Funnies A Carnival Of Comics	57	Sharp Comics #2	158
Fantastic Comics #1	87	Showcase #10	151
The Fantastic Four #3	187	Showcase #13	138
Fantasy Masterpieces #7	228	Showcase #22	284
Feature Funnies #3	236	Showcase #23	169
The Flame #1	185	Single Series #2	127
Forbidden Worlds #82	174	Smash Comics #63	127
Fox And The Crow #1	81	Smash Comics #67	206
Funny Picture Stories #2	217	Special Edition Comics #1	69
Ghost Rider #16	94,125	Spy Cases #26	131
Giant Comics Editions #11	238	Star Comics V2#6	211
Gorgo #2	279	Star Comics V2#7	215
Green Lantern #1	108	Star Ranger Funnies V2#5	204
Hopalong Cassidy #3	240	Star Spangled Comics #1	212
Jackie Gleason/Honeymooners #1	267	Star Spangled Comics #10	129,204
John Wayne Adventure Comics #9	112	Star Spangled Comics #12	197
Journey Into Mystery #1	162	Star Spangled Comics #54	202
Journey Into Mystery #19	163	Star Trek #21	126
Journey Into Mystery #56	208	Straight Arrow #7	78
Journey Into Mystery #97	166	Strange Adventures #21	46
Justice League Of America #9	123	Strange Tales #81	95
King Comics #3	245	Strange Tales #93	52
Manhunt #14 (A-1 #77)	242	Strange Worlds #5	79
March of Comics #42	35	Sub-Mariner Comics #12	158
Marge's Little Lulu #15	37	Super Comics #74	256
Marvel Mystery #16	92	Super Duck #9	164
Marvel Mystery Comics #11	222	Superman #3	157
Marvel Mystery Comics #32	282	Superman #53	71
Marvel Tales #93	179	Superman #57	105
Master Comics #11	254	Superman #169	209
Metal Men #21	281	Superman's Girl Friend Lois Lane #63	259
Mickey Mouse #31	290	Superman's Pal, Jimmy Olsen #87	275
Mickey Mouse Magazine #7	214	Super Mystery Comics V6#2	251
My Friend Irma #36	161	Sure-Fire Comics #3	89
My Greatest Adventure #40	226	Suzie #53	198
My Greatest Adventure #51	252	Tales Of The Unexpected #40	286
My Little Margie #1	48	Target Comics V2#4	250
My Past Confessions #8	164	Target Comics V2#7	270
Mysteries Of Unexplored Worlds #5	213	Target Comics V10#2	160
Mysterious Adventures #10	207	Tarzan #15	247
Mysterious Suspense #1	210	Tarzan #16	224
Mystery In Space #91	119	Tom Mix Comics #3	124
Mystic Comics #9	124	True Complete Mystery #7	206
Mystical Tales #2	261	Walt Disney's Comics & Stories #76	203
Nellie The Nurse #7	113	Walt Disney's Comics & Stories #123	281
New Book Of Comics #2	136	Walt Disney's Comics & Stories #149	210
New Comics #11	232	Walt Disney's Comics & Stories #153	165
Northwest Mounties #12	274	Walt Disney's Comics & Stories #210	285
The Original Ghost Rider #4	122	W. Disney's D. Duck in Disneyland #1	39
Our Fighting Forces #12	272	War Action #13	280
Police Comics #44	200	Web Of Evil #6	161
Police Comics #71	280	Weird Comics #1	59
Prize Comics #7	263	Western Hero #110	265
Real Screen Comics #34	145,199	Western Tales of Black Rider #30	50
Red Rabbit Comics #14	289	World's Finest Comics #10	154
Red Ryder #1	61	World's Finest Comics #113	230
Red Ryder Comics #53	254	Zip-Jet #1	220